MW01228666

DEAL WITH THE HURTS
OR THE HURTS WILL DEAL WITH YOU
A Twelve-Step Process of Forgiveness
By Michael Byrd, PhD

Contents

To my beautiful, loving wife, I thank you for believing and recognizing the call of God on my life. Without your support, I don't believe I would have had the strength or patience to complete this book.

Acknowledgments

Special thanks goes to my spiritual covering, my father in the gospel, Apostle Michael Stevenson. I also extend much appreciation to my second spiritual father and former pastor, Rev. Elder Millard Harvey Jr., for you encouraged me to go forward in ministry. Thank you, Jill Darden, for the hours of work you spent in production. Last, deep gratitude goes to my two closest friends, William Hollins and Randy Snow. William, though we only talk or see each other two or three times a year, I truly value your friendship. Randy Snow not only served as my high school coach, but he also proved to be a true friend and mentor throughout the years. I love you all! I am who I am because of the positive impact you have had on my life. Thank you.

Preface

Once in a group for young men on probation, one young man asked me about the African proverb that says, "If you overcome the enemy within, the enemy without can do you no harm!" I explained that it is the past hurts that created the *bitterness* that motivated his unhealthy choices, or the enemy without. Bitterness or resentment and hostility are the enemies within! Young men get pissed off or angry because they feel others are pissing on them, but the reality is that it is what the old folks said, "He is pissing into the wind!" He is his own worst enemy! Young people cannot see how they are hurting themselves, so they blame others. The greater the bitterness, resentment, and hostility, the greater one's impulses are toward unhealthy choices. For some, the hurts motivate them to make unhealthy choices. For others, the hurts drive them to unhealthy choices.

The first step to overcome past hurts is through forgiveness. It is said that unforgiveness is the poison you take to try to hurt someone else. Most people have hurtful issues or baggage that affects the way they interact with others. People who are hurting tend to lash out and hurt those around them. This oftentimes creates a cycle of hurt and counter-hurt that traps people into behaviors that are counterproductive to good relationships. Forgiveness frees them from counterproductive behaviors that rise out of unhealthy choices.

Foreword

Forgiveness, as an interrelated concept among the disciplines of psychology, theology, and spiritual growth, has grown since the 1990s. Christian counselors and clinicians now point to forgiveness as a useful and necessary part of the wounded person's healing process.

Dr. J. M. Brandsma writes in the *Baker Encyclopedia of Psychology and Counseling*, "Forgiveness is overcoming of negative thoughts, feelings, and behaviors not by denying the offense or the right to be hurt or angry, but by viewing the offender with acceptance (if not compassion) so that the forgiver can be healed. Forgiveness is not denial or indifference, pardon, reconciliation, condoning, excusing, passive forgetting, weakness, or an interpersonal game. Forgiveness in no way cancels the crime, but it works to take care of the distortions caused by the unhealthy aspects of anger and resentment so that the person may achieve peace of mind and body."

How to forgive is the big question. In this work, Michael has imparted revelation truth in a simple and organized format that will be extremely helpful. Now, with the introduction of Michael's book, forgiveness focus groups can become a reality. The work is biblical, powerful, and much needed in the kingdom of God. The ministry and their laity are both crippled by the plague of unforgiveness. Marriages fail; churches crumble; and lives are eventually emotionally destroyed because of unforgiveness. Washed up on the beaches of rescue missions and the streets of our large cities are mentally impaired people who were drowned in the sea of unforgiveness. May God bless and use Michael's book to set many Christians free.

Paul W. Carlin, ThD, PhD
The Therapon Institute

Introduction

I would like to start this book at the end of your life. Imagine that after your life, you're standing before the Creator. We all will stand before God to give an account for the things we have done in our lives. We will be responsible for the choices we make, be they bad or good, choices that hurt people or choices that helped people.

Second Corinthians 5:10, "For we must all appear before the judgment seat of Christ that every one may receive the things done in his body, according to that he hath done, whether it be good or bad." The motivation or reason we made those choices will be irrelevant. We will not be rewarded or punished for the motivations or reasons for our choices. Reward or punishment will only come from our actions and our choices. It is vital that we deal with our past hurts and learn to move beyond them so the hurt will not provoke us to hurt others. In our lives now, we rationalize and justify our hurtful behaviors, but on that day, we will realize that all our rationalizations and justifications had been nailed to the cross. We are left with our blood-washed sins or our sins or our acts of love.

This book will talk about people in my years of counseling with hurtful issues and how they hurt others and/or themselves. I will also discuss steps that have helped people overcome those past hurtful issues. In conducting marriage and family counseling, I have found that most of people's problems come from unforgiveness. People develop anger control problems because of unresolved hurts. People develop drug problems trying to deal with past hurt. People go from one bad relationship to the next bad relationship trying to work through past hurts. Divorce is not God's plan. Jeremiah 29:11 shows us God's plan: "For I know the plans I have for you. Says the Lord! They are plans for good, and not disaster, to give you a future and a hope" (NLT). But Satan has plans also. John 10:10 states, "The thief cometh not, but for to steal, and to kill, and to destroy: I am come that they might have life, and that they might have it more abundantly" (KJV). It seems as if Satan is trying to torture people to death.

Tell me if this sounds familiar. A person goes into a store or restaurant. kills everyone, and then kills himself. An interviewer interviews people who knew the killer. They say, "He was so quiet. I do not believe he could do such a thing." Some people carry around the hurts until they can no longer hold it in any further. Noncrazy people do crazy things because of hurts. More and more people are walking around with chips on their shoulders. People with chips on their shoulders can always say that someone else started it. They justify hurting others by saying, "They started it! That's why I hit, stabbed, or shot the other person." People who play the blame game never acknowledge their faults.

When I was growing up, if my friends and I wanted to fight someone, we would put a chip on our shoulder and dare the person to knock it off. Today a guy will get within inches of the other person's face, causing the other person to push him away. Or two girls who want to fight one another will call the other the B-word to provoke her to attack. Their seeming need to be hardcore is linked to their self-identity development. Some youth would rather have a negative identity than no identity at all. Young people challenge one another to find their pecking order as to find their value in a group. The old folks called it "a pissing contest." Youth feel they have to do things more outrageous to get the attention they feel they need. In some communities, the outrageous behaviors are spinning out of control.

One may ask the question, "Is mental illness contagious?" At first you may say, "No way, mental illness is not airborne or contagious by touch." On the other hand, teachers in our inner city as well as others who work with inner city youth see that one kid doing something crazy causes others to act out in crazy ways.

I conduct family counseling and anger-control groups for young people on probation for gang violence as well as other violent crimes. During these sessions, I have found that you can teach clients the most effective tools and skills for controlling their anger, but if they are not given a way of resolving past hurts and resentments, the clients will continue to have problems controlling their anger. They transfer the anger and hurts from the past to a new individual. Treating the anger is treating the symptom. The anger is a symptom of a disease; the disease itself is the past hurt or resentment. In psychology it is called transference.

Webster's defines *transference* as the process by which emotions and desires originally associated with one person, such as a parent or sibling, are unconsciously shifted to another person, especially to the analyst. You can see this when you ask a young child why he/she hit or hurt his/her younger brother/sister. The child will look at you with a blank face and say, "I don't know!" The child doesn't know how to express his/her hurts. Thus the name of this book*, Deal with the Hurts or the Hurts will Deal with You! Hurt people hurt others, and/or they hurt themselves.* The same is true for bitter Christians; the unresolved hurts create an attitude of bitterness. Although they are new creatures in Christ, their actions can continue to be motivated by past hurts. I also have found that many times anger is a secondary emotion or the symptom of a disease. The disease itself is the distress and resentment manifesting from unresolved hurts. I have helped people find healing through the process of learning to forgive and move past the pain.

Once people learn that I conduct anger-control groups for kids on probation, I often hear them say that young people today are angrier and more violent than ever before. Statistics seem to show a trend of growing juvenile violent crimes in our world today, more then ever before. I believe it is difficult for youth to create a good future when they are living and reliving the hurts of the past. Pushing down those feelings of the past seems to cause them to resurface counterproductively in one's present and future. I believe the remedy to the increasing violence is learning to forgive. I believe that this twelve-step process of forgiveness can help individuals, as well as society, decrease violence and bring healing to the land.

The Premise of This Book

Deal with the past hurts, or the hurts will deal with you. People who are hurting hurt other people, or they hurt themselves. Forgiveness is the best way to move beyond one's past hurts. Webster defines forgiveness as, "To cease to feel resentment against on the account of wrong committed." These twelve steps help people move beyond or cease to feel resentment. I will share stories of how people did not deal with their hurts and how their hurts dealt with them.

It is important to understand that one's unresolved hurts and unforgiveness injures oneself more than it hurts the person toward whom one has unforgiveness. If one will not forgive a person for wrongdoing, it does not hold back the person one will not forgive. On the contrary, it holds back the person who will not forgive. People who will not forgive will unconsciously sabotage themselves. People will unconsciously put themselves in positions that allow circumstances to hold them back. The Bible addresses this issue in Proverbs 4:23, which reads, *"Keep thy heart with all diligence; for out of it are the issues of life."* (The Hebrew word for heart means feelings). These negative feelings or emotions destroy one's future. One's negative feelings cause negative actions, which cause negative behaviors and lifestyles. The New Living Translation Bible says, "Guard your heart above all else, for it determines the course of your life." Jesus Christ described it this way in Luke 6:45: "A good man out of the good treasure of his heart [emotions] bringeth forth that which is good; and an evil man out of the evil treasure of his heart bringeth forth that which is evil: for out of the abundance of the heart his mouth speaketh." I believe our "issues of life" or what some people call one's "baggage" are the things that we "bringeth forth" from the unresolved hurt and unforgiveness in our lives. Which direction is your life going? Is it going in a positive direction or a negative direction?

I believe that this book of forgiveness can benefit not only Christians but non-Christians as well! I have worked with both Christians and non-Christians and have seen forgiveness transform their lives. Many people at first believe the old saying that you have to forgive and forget. The reality is that forgetting is counterproductive to forgiving. Forgetting many times becomes suppression or repression. Repressed emotions are a major factor in the development of neurosis and other self-defeating, self-sabotaging psychological problems. Unforgiveness can psychologically enslave people to behaviors that are counterproductive. When a person acknowledges that he or she has been victimized, it helps him or her to break the chains of psychological slavery.

One of the clearest examples I have seen of psychological slavery is the time when a father and stepmother called and asked me to see their daughter because they thought she was a kleptomaniac. The daughter would go to the store with money and credit cards but steal things for no reason other than the impulse to take. She would also steal things from family members and friends. She would constantly say, "I didn't know that I took those things!" She had repressed the hurt of her parents taking away her childhood, apparently by moving her back and forth during their separation and divorce. Her repressed hurt feelings from her stolen childhood were expressing themselves counterproductively through her subconscious impulse to take things.

Why Should We Forgive?

Many of my clients at first believe that forgiveness is a sign of weakness. They believe that if you forgive transgressions, then transgressions will continue. If you allow people to step on you once, they will continue to walk over you. I encourage my clients to see the truth—that forgiveness is a sign of strength and courage. It takes no courage to lash out or hold onto hurt and unforgiveness. On the contrary, it takes great courage to forgive. Many of them have believed that retaliation is the best way, if not the only way, of dealing with past hurts and resentments. Retaliation does not remove the pain from past hurts. It does, on the other hand, magnify it; it shines more light on the hurt so that it may be clearly seen. Retaliation does not remove the pain from the past hurts. Retaliation causes one to focus on the hurt and to think about it more, thereby increasing the ill feelings.

As a conflict mediator and trainer of conflict mediators, retaliation and revenge have been discouraged as a way to resolve conflicts because they can escalate conflict, leading to a reciprocal chain of revenge and counter-revenge that may last for weeks, months, or in the case of racism, even generations.

Retaliation does not cancel the pain, but it reinforces the pain and resentment of what caused the unforgiveness. Retaliation does try to compensate for hurts by causing hurt to others, and one may have an initial sense of satisfaction but later have to deal with feelings of guilt as well as the hurt and resentment from the unresolved issue. Forgiveness, in fact, always involves an apparent short-term loss for a real long-term gain. Violence and retaliation are the exact opposite. Retaliation gives the short-term gain of temporary feelings of satisfaction at the cost of long-term pain and discontentment. If we are really honest with ourselves, we will be able to recall a time when we held in hurts or anger and later took them out on someone who did not deserve it.

I have learned that there really is a divine design to every experience, and no matter how painful, these experiences are reflections of something we need to know about ourselves. If we really dig, we are bound to find out something we can use to our own benefit. (I will explain this more in the section, "The Purpose behind the Pain.") I like thinking of our lives as a picture or portrait of ourselves. In life, the events that make up your life are parts of the picture, and together they bring clarity to your portrait. When a person works through hurt and unforgiveness, it makes that event in the portrait clearer, more vivid, and a more perfect representation of the image of that person's life. Forgetting or repressing the hurt and resentment leaves a blank spot in your portrait. Unforgiveness magnifies the problem, thereby making that part of the picture out of proportion to the rest of the picture. If a person stays in unforgiveness, it makes the picture fuzzy and unclear, thereby making it unattractive. When a person retaliates, it gives the picture an out-of-proportion image, and the picture's symmetry is off center, leaving that event in the person's picture of life seemingly unbalanced or warped.

Forgiveness is not only good for the person who is forgiven but also for the person who forgives. Since forgiveness means freeing you to love, you will feel in love with your true self and with other people's real selves when you forgive. Other people will feel that you love them and will love you in return. It's in your self-interest to forgive because you will be better off.

Unforgiveness not only causes emotional sickness, but it causes physical illness as well. Studies have found that people who were able to forgive a person who had hurt them had fewer chronic illnesses than those who could not forgive. Forgiveness also helps the heart. When people talked about being betrayed by a loved one, their blood pressure and heart rates increased. Researchers have noted the numbers dropped when the subjects talked about resolving the problem but stayed high when they didn't want to forgive. Facts have shown that giving up a grudge may be powerful enough to change your outlook on life. A study found that incest survivors who learned to forgive their offenders were able to develop normal levels of self-esteem and hope, while those who could not forgive remained depressed. Those researchers believe forgiveness may release unexpressed anger. Staying in unforgiveness can cause your body to produce adrenaline, while levels of serotonin, the mood-boosting brain chemical, dip. They speculate that over time, this combination may put a damper on your immune system.

Holding a grudge may deplete your resources to fight and/or recuperate from illness. Experts believe that letting go of unforgiveness can help relieve the stress so you're better able to cope with illness. Other studies have shown that holding onto anger may increase your chances of a heart attack as well as cancer, high blood pressure, high cholesterol, and other illnesses.

When I speak at conferences and workshops, I often hear reports and testimonies of healing from incurable diseases once people forgive. Forgiveness boosts your self-esteem and lowers your blood pressure and heart rate, experts say. From my experience, I personally believe that forgiveness may also help you sleep better at night and boost a positive change in your attitude. Another study in which an individuals' emotional states were measured found that before and after they had forgiven someone who had hurt them, they no longer had feelings of anxiety and depression and felt better about themselves. I believe that unforgiveness turned inward causes health problems and psychological problems. I believe unforgiveness turned outward can lead to anger problems, which can cause legal and relationship problems. You have to deal with the hurt or the hurt will deal with you, because people who are hurting hurt others and themselves.

As a Christian therapist, I see young people with great potential but who sabotage their future because of past hurts. I see married people who really love each other get divorced because of past hurts. I see people in the church who love God but hate their Christian brothers or sisters because of past hurts. My main reason for preaching and teaching about this is because hurts and unforgiveness toward a person destroys love for that person. Realizing we have only one commandment to love God and love one another, our love for God can only be seen through our love for one another. One's unforgiveness destroys one's love for others. Unforgiveness creates bitterness and resentment, which not only hinders relationship with the person you have the unforgiveness toward but also hinders all other relationships.

Some Christians believe we cannot receive answers to prayers if we have unforgiveness. They base this belief on Mark 11:24–25, where the writer gives two requirements to receiving answers to prayers: (1) That you believe that you will receive it. (2) When you pray, if you hold anything against anyone, you must forgive that person. This also corresponds to Mark 6:37–38, "Forgive and ye shall be forgiven: Give, and it shall be given unto you; good measure…"

The most important reason to forgive is to be like Jesus! The disciples were first called Christians (or Christlike) in Antioch (Acts 11:26).

Today people wear rubber bands or t-shirts with, "WWJD, What Would Jesus Do?" Jesus would love! And Jesus would forgive!

Twelve-Step Process of Forgiveness

Step One. Admit that you have hurts and/or unforgiveness toward someone or a situation and that unforgiveness has caused problems for yourself and/or others.

Step Two. Make a searching and fearless moral inventory of yourself for hurts and unforgiveness.

Step Three. Make a decision to forgive.

Step Four. Be ready to allow God to help you in the forgiving process.

Step Five. Clarify the issue(s) of unforgiveness

Step Six. Empathize with the person or situation that caused the unforgiveness if you can, and/or reframe the past.

Step Seven. Pray for the person or situation for which you have unforgiveness.

Step Eight. Practice affirmations of forgiveness.

Step Nine. Take a forgiveness inventory. Imagine the person(s) or situation in your mind toward which you have unforgiveness for twenty seconds.

A. If you have feelings of happiness and/or best wishes for the person or situation, go to step ten.

B. If you have feelings of pain, hurt, or resentment, then go back to step three.

Step Ten. Be ready to forgive as issues and situations come up.

Step Eleven. Continue to take an inventory.

Step Twelve. Experience a spiritual awakening—a stronger relationship with God, others, and yourself.

Step One

Admit you have hurts and/or unforgiveness toward someone or a situation and that the unforgiveness has caused problems for yourself and/or others. We have to admit, not forget. In the traditional equation, forgiveness plus forgetting brings healing. Counselors and psychologists have a surprising answer: you don't forget. They say the journey toward forgiveness starts with remembering, not forgetting. You must acknowledge your hurt, and then you can work to release it.

A psychologist I once worked with said, "A person is only as sick as the secrets they keep." One's secrets make one's sickness grow. When I first began doing counseling with people, I became nervous when, in long-term counseling, the client shared a secret that made me say, "Ah! Now I understand the hurt that is driving that self-sabotaging behavior." Now when I am doing long-term therapy, I only become nervous when people don't share the secret that is driving their self-sabotaging behavior. So, too, is one's unforgiveness. When one tries to hide the hurt, it seems to have a bigger effect on how one interacts with others. If you don't try to talk about things, it will be difficult to have a relationship with others.

It's as if your hurt feelings from one relationship poison your ability to connect with other people. In counseling singles with unforgiveness, many report that hurt in early relationships seem to revisit them in later relationships (transference), as if they are attracting people who will hurt them in the same way (they are unconsciously sabotaging their future).

One example of this is once in marriage counseling, I worked with a couple who continued to sabotage their relationship/marriage. Both of them were devoted, Spirit-filled Christians. One had remarried three times, the other four times before marrying each other. Both of them had hurtful issues from prior relationships that affected how they interacted with one another. His issue was trust because he had been betrayed several times in pervious relationships. Her issues were control and manipulation, stemming from abuse. Her attempts to control and manipulate would push her husband away, causing him to believe she was manipulating him so she could be with other people. Ironically, knowing that he had trust issues, she tried to use that to control him.

We all have issues we need to deal with. I also found in self-analysis (looking at my actions and their unconscious motives) that I sometimes choose passive-aggressive behavior to deal with personal hurt. For example, sometimes when someone hurts me and apologizes, I dismiss the apology and do not admit to him or her and to myself that what the person did hurt me. I might also say to the person that what he or she did, did not matter (it had no effect on me). Then later I unconsciously say or do things to hurt and/or get back at the person. This, of course, unconsciously sabotages my future with that person. I have had to recognize in myself that, although I may say, "We are okay," the reality is that I had unforgiveness toward that person. I had to admit to myself that I had unforgiveness and then consciously forgive the person.

The first step for many people is the hardest step to make. Some people do not have the courage to admit to themselves, and even less to another person, that they have hurts and unforgiveness in their lives. Other people live in denial; like addicts, they deny that they have a problem, that the hurt exists, or that it ever happened (repression). If one does not use the emotional energy it takes to admit that there is a problem, one will not use the emotional energy it takes to try and fix the problem, thereby allowing the problem to affect more and more of one's life.

Early in my ministry, I worked in a church with a Christian brother who was raising his ten-year-old son and fourteen-year-old daughter. He was wheelchair-bound, suffering from multiple sclerosis (MS). In the presence of his children, he would often insult his ex-wife for running off and leaving him to raise the two kids. His bitterness was obvious to everyone but not to himself. In talking to him about forgiveness, he would say, "I forgive her, but I cannot forget how she misused me…" He would then go into a story of how she had hurt him. The words that came out of his mouth revealed what was truly in his heart. I felt helpless to help him see his unforgiveness. It was obvious that he was repressing his hurt from the experience. He could not admit to himself that he had unforgiveness toward his ex-wife. His unforgiveness was not only hurting him but his kids as well.

By talking about his ex-wife (their mother) in front of his kids, he did not realize he was poisoning the water he was going to have to drink from in the future. He later did not understand why his kids became rebellious. He did not know that by speaking and causing distrust toward their mother, he was speaking and causing distrust toward himself. Matthews 15:11 says, "Not that which goeth into the mouth defileth a man; but that which cometh out of the mouth, this defileth a man." What he was saying about his ex-wife was reinforcing the pain, causing the anger he felt about her to grow (or defile him) His words not only affected the way he felt but how his kids felt as well.

Admitting is the first step to forgiveness. Without it, the healing process cannot begin. As I stated before, some believe that, without forgiveness, there is no healing. Being able to talk about it seems sometimes unimportant. If you don't try to talk about things, it will be difficult to have a relationship with others. It is as if one's hurt feelings from past relationships interfere with one's ability to connect with other people in the present. People question why they seem to attract people they cannot get along with, like a person trying to force a round peg through a triangle.

People sometimes manipulate others to react to them in the way they feel they deserve to be treated. The reality is that, unconsciously, they are sabotaging their relationship. I have counseled with abuse survivors who

17

had found other relationships where they pushed and pushed the person in the new relationship until that person also became abusive to them. I have conducted counseling with girls who have hit, scratched, and yelled, "Hit me... go ahead, hit me!" to new boyfriends, as if to reinforce their belief that they deserved to be abused. They act like people who shake the Coke bottle before opening it and then question why the Coke explodes on them. They would blame the boyfriend, not seeing their part in the problem.

Once they work through the forgiving process, it seems to free them to find someone who will respect them because now they respect themselves. I have found that sometimes just having patients talk about it helps to bring healing. Once, in counseling with a seventeen-year-old student, as she talked, she continued to cover her face and forehead or hold her stomach with her hand. She said that she had not been eating, that she did not like her family, and that she had been thinking about killing herself.

I asked her, "What ways have you thought about to kill yourself?"

She said, "Last week I tried to kill myself by taking some pills before going to bed, the next morning I woke up, I was mad that nothing happened."

I then empathically explained that, by law, I have to report when a student states that he/she has or will hurt him/herself or someone else. I explained that I would have to let her grandmother know about the suicidal attempt. (The girl's grandmother had guardianship over her.) She continued, "I just wanted to end it all." I asked what kind of pills she took. She said, "I don't know." I asked where she had gotten them, and she said, "I got them from my doctor last week... He said if I don't have surgery, I will not live to see eighteen years old."

I asked how her grandmother felt about the surgery. She said, "She doesn't know." I again explained that I would have to let her grandmother know about the doctor's report. She looked down, nodded, and said, "I know." We continued to talk as we tried to contact her grandmother. She began to pour out her story—her unspeakable feelings, her anger and unforgiveness toward her mother.

I told her a story about a former student who, from his perspective, had a right to live in unforgiveness. When he was in elementary school, he witnessed his father being murdered. He said, "I will never forgive him," speaking of his father's killer. His unforgiveness and anger at his father's killer caused him to be in constant trouble in school and with the law. He would often get into fights for the smallest of reasons. He, like many people, transferred his anger to others. His anger kept him from learning to read and do well in school. I said that unforgiveness does not hold back the person you're angry with; it only holds back you, the person who will not forgive. She began to try to justify her unforgiveness toward her mother. I said that the former student justified his anger as well, but it still held him back.

As she began to confess her forgiveness, using affirmations, she began to sit more and more erect and stopped holding her stomach and head. I saw her countenance change in front of me. She seemed to become healed as we spoke. I said, "You are beginning to look different. You are not holding your stomach or covering your face. How do you feel?" After a pause, she replied, "Well, I still feel something in my stomach, but I guess okay!" In one of our later sessions, I learned that she had a follow-up visit with her doctor, and he now believes she will no longer need the surgery. Once she was able to admit to her unforgiveness, she was able to begin the forgiving and healing process.

When people push down the hurts of the past, many times those hurt feelings cause them to explode in their present or future! Admitting you have hurts or unforgiveness toward someone or a situation is the first and most important step to take; that is why I am convinced that, without forgiveness, the healing process cannot begin.

Step Two

Make a searching and fearless moral inventory of yourself for hurts and unforgiveness. For some, it is hard to forgive someone in the present because they have unforgiveness of someone similar in the past. Some people can't forgive all black people, white people, and/or Hispanics because someone of that race before has hurt them. In most twelve-step programs, the members believe in this step. They have learned the importance of a personal inventory. This is Step Four in the Alcohol Anonymous/ Narcotics Anonymous programs. The members sometime use an illustration of a business that, if it did not take regular inventory, would usually go broke. In a commercial inventory taking are a fact-finding and a fact-facing process. It is in an effort to discover the truth about the stock-in-trade.

The purpose is to disclose damaged or unsalvageable goods, to get rid of them without regret. If we are the owners of a business and if it is going to be successful, we cannot fool ourselves about its value. If we look at our lives as a business and would like our business to be successful, we need to do exactly the same thing with our lives. We should take an honest inventory. First, we need to search out the flaws in our makeup that cause our failure. The fact is that our hurts manifest themselves in various ways that sabotage our lives. I believe that the biggest manifestations are unforgiveness and resentment. From these stem most forms of illness, for we have not only been mentally and physically ill, but we have also been spiritually sick. When the spiritual malady is overcome, we straighten out mentally and physically. In dealing with unforgiveness and resentments, we need to set them on paper (See forgiveness list on pages 66–67.) Identify and write down the people or incidents in your life that you need to forgive. Choose one person at a time, and apply the twelve-step process to each in incident.

We need to list the people and institutions with whom we were angry and/or hurt. On our unforgiveness and resentments list, we set opposite each name our injuries and how we felt. Because it is so easy for us to discount unforgiven feelings, it is important to write them down. Discounting those feelings or blowing them off does not make them go away or make their unconscious responses to unforgiveness less likely to become self-defeating, self-sabotaging behaviors. Pushing down one's hurt feelings of the past is like pushing the plunger that causes the explosion in one's present and/or future. People who blow-up for no reason really do have a reason, that being unforgiveness. Thus you have to examine yourself. You can ask young people why they hit their brother/sister. They often respond, "I don't know why!" They don't know why they are motivated to give hurt. It is their past hurts. Today we can see a lot of people hurting others for seemingly no reason! This is not to say that unforgiveness is the only cause of all life's problems. Rather, I like to show the self-defeating, self-sabotaging impact of unforgiveness on one's life.

One example is this couple I knew before they were married. She knew of her husband's great hatred and anger toward his mother. Four years into their marriage, she was talking divorce. She said, "His blowing up for no reason is now affecting my daughter. I can't let her grow up under so much anger." I told her that he was trying to work through his anger and resentment toward his mother (transference). I also told her that she knew that the husband would demand joint custody of the daughter and that if he did not work through his anger with her, he would be trying to work through it with the next woman and her daughter would still be exposed and affected by his anger. I also told her that he could become healed through finding the unconditional love he was looking for from his mother.

In counseling, counselors readily address the displays of self-defeating and self-sabotaging behaviors but many times overlook the root of past hurts and unforgiveness. We must take inventory of unforgiveness in our lives to break the cycle of self-defeating and self-sabotaging behaviors. Make a searching and fearless moral inventory of yourself for hurts and unforgiveness. Step two is one of the most important steps to healing, for psychology says that we have a blind spot when looking at ourselves. We often overlook our faults and shortcomings or issues/baggage, but we see other people's faults and shortcomings with crystal clarity. Jesus said, "Worry about a speck in your brother's eye when you have a log in your eye." Thus we have to search our hearts for the motivations behind our actions. Are my actions motivated by love and concern or anger, hatred, and resentment?

Step Three

Make a decision to forgive, to heal, and to let your desire for peace become greater than your anger, pursuit of revenge, or need for some kind of compensation. Make a clean break. If you choose to let go, just let it go.

Don't permit your mind to replay again and again an experience that dishonored or violated you. Resolve to move on. This doesn't mean you deny your feelings. It means you don't get stuck in them. It's not that you don't care; just the opposite. For me, moving on means you care for yourself enough to realize that you have the power to change your mind (thinking and feeling). I am talking about a commitment to resolve in yourself to do something about it, not just think about it or be angry about it. Every time you think about the situation, work the steps of forgiveness.

James 4:17 says, "Therefore to him that knoweth to do good, and doeth [it] not, to him it is sin." For one to know that one needs to forgive is not good enough. We have to make that decision to forgive and follow through. I sometimes ask my clients, "How do you eat an elephant?" The answer is, "One bite at a time!" Just to think about eating an elephant seems overwhelming; one may think that one will choke because of its enormity; so, too, forgiveness at times seems enormous! Making a decision to forgive is like taking that first bite. Once you have taken that first bite, the other bites become easier and easier.

Blaming

In the introduction, I talked about people walking around with chips on their shoulders, waiting for someone to knock them off. Unfortunately, people try to deal with past hurts by blaming others. They blame others for the troubles they create. I personally know of young people who are so angry and distrustful (chips on their shoulders) toward their teachers that they don't learn the things they need to go to the next level.

I personally know of people who are continuously in and out of jail or prison because of the chips on their shoulders, but they always have someone to blame for their incarceration. When you blame someone, you give him or her the power over your life! When we blame people, we make them responsible for our actions/behaviors.

If I blame my sister for not teaching me to tie my shoe and choose to remain unknowledgeable in that area, my sister indirectly controls what goes on my feet. If I blame my brother for not teaching me to drive and I choose to not learn another way, then because I don't know how to drive, he indirectly controls where I go. If I blame my mother for not teaching me to read, she indirectly controls what I can learn. If I blame my father for not teaching me how to treat a woman, he indirectly controls how I treat my wife. If I blame someone for what I can or can't do, I give him or her the power over what I can and can't do.

People want the role and responsibility of the boss but won't take responsibility for the small things that go wrong in life. If a person can't take responsibility for the small things in life, how can he or she take responsibility over the larger things in life? You can't be the boss if you can't be responsible; you can't be responsible if you blame others! Making a decision to forgive is not blaming the person for the hurts but taking responsibility for how you feel and moving on.

There was a song we sang in church taken from Exodus 14:14, "The Lord shall fight for you, and ye shall hold your peace." The song said, "If I hold my peace and let the Lord fight my battles Victory! Victory shall be mine!" We want the victory, but we want to fight our own battles! If we want to win, we need God's help!

Young men get pissed off or angry because they feel others are pissing on them, but the reality is that they are pissing in the wind! They are their own worst enemies! They can't see how they are hurting themselves, so they blame others. Proverbs 25:21–22 says, "If thine enemy be hungry give him bread to eat; and if thine enemy be thirsty give him water to drink. For thou shalt heap coals of fire upon his head, and the Lord shall reward thee." In working with young people in gangs, I have seen that they create their own enemy. If your enemy is hungry, give him food! They say, "No! He deserves to be hungry!" And if your enemy is thirsty, give him water! They say, "No! He doesn't deserve water to drink." They blame other groups of people for the problems they create. They say, "They don't deserve mercy."

Some Christians are only nice to get back at others to "heap coals of fire upon his head." If we are only being nice to others to hurt them, you have resentment in your heart." I remind the reader of several scriptures. The first is in Proverbs 4:23, which reads, "Keep thy heart with all diligence; for out of it are the issues of life." Blaming is saying things to justify our anger.

Job 2:9–10 says, "His wife said to him are you still holding on to your integrity? Curse God and die! He replied, you are talking like a foolish woman. Shall we accept good from God, and not trouble? In *all this Job did not sin in what he said"* (NIV). So what did Job say while going through his trouble? Job 5:19–26 says:

He will deliver thee in six troubles; Yea, in seven there shall no evil touch thee. In famine he will redeem thee from death; And in war from the power of the sword. Thou shalt be hid from the scourge of the tongue; Neither shalt thou be afraid of destruction when it cometh. At destruction and dearth thou shalt laugh; Neither shalt thou be afraid of the beasts of the earth. For thou shalt be in league with the stones of the field; And the beasts of the field shall be at peace with thee. And thou shalt know that thy tent is in peace; And thou shalt visit thy fold, and shalt miss nothing. Thou shalt know also that thy seed shall be great, And thine offspring as the grass of the earth. Thou shalt come to thy grave in a full age, Like as a shock of grain cometh in its season (ASV).

Job 13:15 also says, "Though He slay me yet will I trust Him…" Job did not blame God. Job only spoke words of faith and trust in God.

Unfortunately blaming can become a way of life. Some people always make excuses or blame others for failing before they fail. I have had students one-third or one-fourth of the way through one class blame the drama they have to deal with at home for the reason why they are going to fail the class. For most of those students, blaming has become a way of life. Some students feel unworthy of receiving good things. If you don't think you are worthy of receiving good things, chances are you won't receive them. If you do receive good things and you think you don't deserve them, most likely you will find some way of sabotaging it.

Divorced men and women blame their ex-spouses for their divorce. This may be hard to believe, but I have found hardened criminals blame their victims for their crime. I have heard rapists blame their victims' clothes for raping them. Robbers blame their victims' fighting back for the reason they killed them. Gang members blame the deceased rival gang member for killing him/her. Like racists of old, they say he/she is now a good blank gang member. Gangsters kill people for telling the truth. They call it killing a snitch! Some people blame God. If a person can justify his sin he/she will continue in that sin! We all have to control our passions, or our passions will control us! One of the hardest hurts to deal with is guilt and shame of the past.

As a black male counselor, I have experienced on three different occasions of counseling Caucasian students coming to talk to me about how they felt regarding the unfairness of life. They believed it was minorities, specifically blacks and Hispanics, keeping them from getting good jobs or getting into college. The first two times this happened, I felt like I had to explain the history of racism, realizing that the only reasons why my head is above the sewage of life is because of God and the shoulders I am standing on of the people who have sacrificed their lives so I can have a better life. They seemed to remain bitter and continued to blame.

The third time a white student came and talked to me about how he felt about his believed plight in life and his belief that it was because of the blacks and Hispanics, I refocused his thinking on his choices to control his future. I tried to help him realize that by blaming others, he was limiting himself. As long as he had someone to blame, he did not have to take responsibility for his future. We talked about the fact that he could not be successful unless he was responsible. Also, he was not being responsible for himself as long as he was blaming others. I personally believe God wants us to be successful, so the only person that can hold you back is yourself. But we unknowingly hold ourselves back by blaming others. We, like the

24

children of Israel, have a promise but don't receive the promise when we blame others.

Step Four

Be ready to allow God to help you in the forgiving process. Some people are offended by the term higher power, but if it is easier for the reader to use the term higher power, go right ahead. In working with non-Christians, I explain to them that I am not asking them to commit their life to Christ but only to allow God to help them. Some of our hurts are so painful that we need help to overcome them. Some people go to a physician; others go to a counselor.

I direct people to the master physician, the master counselor. But in many cases, allowing God to help them to forgive leads them to trusting God, which may also lead to a commitment to Christ.

Some of our hurts we cannot heal without help. I believe God will show us how to take a kindly and tolerant view of each and every one. The question you may ask is, how can you forgive when your emotional injury may range from an occasion where a friend jokingly hurts you to a spouse's betrayal or even to the lingering resentment over societal injustices, such as slavery and racial discrimination? When you've been hurt, how do you turn the other cheek and act as if nothing happened? If we follow the teaching and example of Jesus, Christians believe that mercy is received by giving mercy. Believers must be people of mercy because a God who is love showed mercy to us. The God who enters into history to redeem us, and through the dramatic events of the cross prepares the victory of Resurrection Sunday, is a God of mercy and forgiveness. Thus, Jesus told those who challenged his dining with sinners, "Go and learn what this means, I desire mercy and not sacrifice, for I came not to call the righteous, but sinners" (Matt. 9:13). The followers of Christ who are baptized into his redeeming death and resurrection must always be men and women of mercy and forgiveness. I will never apologize to anyone for depending upon our Creator.

There are those who think spirituality is the way of weakness. Paradoxically, I see it as the way of strength. In history we see that the people of faith were people of courage. All men and women of faith have courage. They trust their God. I will never apologize for believing in God. Instead I permit him to demonstrate his love and forgiveness through me. If we ask him to remove our weaknesses and direct us to be what he would have us to be, I believe we can begin to outgrow our weaknesses. We asked God to mold us and help us to live up to what he would have us be. If we do not allow God to help us forgive, we will continue in self-sabotaging behaviors. The reality is that our troubles are, for the most part, of our own making. Remember Luke 6:45 says, "A good man out of the good treasure of his heart bringeth forth that which is good; and an evil man out of the evil treasure of his heart bringeth forth that which is evil: for out of the abundance of the heart his mouth speaketh." Our problems arise out of selfishness and self-sabotaging behaviors. They are extreme examples of our self-will intensifying, although we blame others for the problems we have created. We need help getting rid of this selfishness (i.e., we must allow God to help).

We must kill selfishness, or it will eventually kill us! Like the Apostle Paul, I die daily! God makes that possible. There often seems no way of entirely getting rid of selfishness without God's aid. Many of us had moral and philosophical convictions, but we could not live up to them even though we would have liked to. Neither could we reduce our self-centeredness much by wishing or trying with our own power. We had to have God's help. So, too, do we need God's help to forgive! Yes! We humbly ask God to help us to forgive ourselves and help us forgive others. Jesus gave us the golden rule: "Do to others as you would like them to do to you or for you." Jesus also talked about people living by the law of nature, "Treat others the same way they treat us!" These people are kind to those who are kind to them and hateful to those who are hateful to them. Some people, in their hyper-vigilance, will try to hurt others before someone can hurt them. They say, "I am going to get them before they can get me!"

The Law of Reciprocity
We have to realize that, for the most part, our troubles are basically of our own making. Like the domino effect, because we have been hurt, we hurt others. That in turn encourages others to hurt us in the future. In the law of reciprocity, *reciprocate* means to give and take mutually, to return in kind (even in another kind) or degree. In layman's terms, "What goes around comes around." This is a very clear principle throughout the Bible, and especially the New Testament. Look at Matthew 7:1–2: "Do not judge, or you too will be judged. For in the same way you judge others, you will be judged, and with the measure you use, it will be measured to you." My childhood pastor said we receive "in kind" what we give away. Luke 6:31, the golden rule, says, "Do to others as you would have them do to you." In other words, treat others how you wish to be treated! Second Corinthians 9:6 says, "Remember this: Whoever sows sparingly will also reap sparingly, and whoever sows generously will also reap generously." If you sow unforgiveness, hate, and violence, you will reap unforgiveness, hate, and violence.

People try to control as much of their environment as possible in order to direct and/or control their future. By cutting the strings of hate and unforgiveness, one frees oneself from reacting in self-sabotaging ways. I have counseled individuals who have lost their jobs because someone they hated and/or had unforgiveness toward said or did something that made them mad (pulled their string like a puppet), which caused them to act inappropriately, which caused them to be fired.

I have counseled students who had unforgiveness toward another student, and because that other student looked at them (pulled their strings) they became so infuriated that they tried to fight the other student, which caused them to be kicked out of school, sabotaging their education and future. I believe people, for the most part, can control how others treat them. For example, if you smile at people, most of them will smile back. The same is true for an angry look. People will give you an angry look back. Have you ever walked into a place tired and sleepy, but someone's warm smile and pleasant personality brightened your day and caused you to smile back to him or her? Or have you ever run into someone whose nasty, angry attitude caused you to get an attitude toward him or her?

It is hard to trust people when you have unforgiveness. It is even harder to give love to someone you don't trust. But we like for people to show love toward us! What goes around comes around. If we want love, we have to give love! The law of reciprocity is true for mercy and forgiveness. Matthew 5:7 states, "Blessed are the merciful, for they will be shown mercy." Matthew 6:15 says, "But if ye forgive not men their trespasses, neither will your Father forgive your trespasses."

The question I ask my students and clients is, "Who do you want to be in control over the direction of your life? Will it be you or someone you hate or toward whom you have unforgiveness?" You have to cut the strings of unforgiveness! For some clients, it seems as if their lives are spinning out of control. I see their lives spinning like water going down the drain; it gets faster and faster as it goes along. I have had people tell me that they feel like their life is being flushed down the drain. I have seen forgiveness used as a way of putting a stop to that downward spiral.

Cut the emotional strings that pull you down or make you react in unhealthy ways. Cut the strings that control what you do and say, thereby controlling your future!

My clients have a hard time believing me when they ask me this hypothetical question, "If someone came up to me and hit me for no reason, would I hit the person back?" I tell them because of the way I treat people, I have created an environment around me that makes that unlikely!

But I admit to them that I once was insecure, and there was a time in my life when the only leg I could stand on was my pride. It was the one thing I could not afford to lose. Now I have more going for me; I have more support and security in my life. I can now afford to lose a little pride to win success! I ask them to imagine that using makeup, you could earn $30,000 in a part playing Dr. Martin Luther King Jr. However, in the audition, a white man acting like a member of the KKK calls you the N-word and hits you. To win the part, your response must be to immediately forgive and turn the other cheek. The question I ask my clients is, "Would it be worth it to lose your pride to win the part? How would a teacher or a preacher handle that part? How would a thug or a gang member handle that part?" They would each handle the challenge differently. The teacher and preacher have a better chance of responding positively to the N-word and being hit than the gang member would. I use this example to illustrate that if people can control their emotional responses (attitude), they can control their destiny. Again I remind my readers of Proverbs 4:23, which says, "Guard your heart above all else, for it determines the course of your life" (NLT). Teachers and preachers have a better chance at controlling their destiny or issues of life than a gang member.

Forgiveness cuts the strings that others use to control your emotions, thereby controlling your actions/behaviors. In the law of reciprocity, what goes around comes around. The thing my clients that are in and out of jail need most in life is mercy! One gets mercy by being merciful. The clients are quick to point out that they do not see how the KKK deserves mercy; I point out that the justice system doesn't see how they deserve mercy.

In the law of reciprocity, you have to give mercy to receive mercy. I was talking with a young man in prison who was upset because he had been passed over a few times for parole. He, like many inmates, believed that showing mercy is showing weakness and that he could not afford to show weakness in the hostile environment of prison. I shared with him that, if he wanted to receive mercy, he needed to be merciful. He was doing everything he believed he needed to do to stay alive, but because he was not willing to show mercy, he was doing the thing that kept him in prison. What goes around comes around. No mercy given, no mercy received.

Many inner-city young people believe the thing that is needed most to make it in life is luck because the people who make it out of the inner cities are lucky! I share with them that I believe luck or good fortune is gained by working hard and taking advantage of good opportunities to better oneself in life.

I remember a passage in George S. Clason's book *The Richest Man in Babylon*. He explains that people look for luck or the goddess of luck at the gambling table or the horse races, where men lose more money than they win. But you find good luck or good fortune in hard work, and work has a surer possibility of reward of good fortune. Where? We receive those famous words of wisdom, "God helps those who help themselves!" In other words, you find luck or good fortune by hard work. I explain that there are many football and basketball players, doctors, and lawyers who come from the inner city. The one thing they have in common is that they worked hard and took advantage of opportunities in front of them to better themselves.

I often ask myself where I would be if I had not competed in gymnastics in a neighborhood where people only played football and basketball. For many people, gymnastics was viewed as a "gay" sport. Real men played basketball or football. Gymnastics forced me to focus on schoolwork so I could compete. If I had not been forced to focus on school, I do not believe I would have graduated from high school. The harder I worked in the gym, the better I placed when competing. But if I goofed off weeks before a meet, I did poorly in that meet. The law of reciprocity application is when I did well in the gym, I performed well in the meet. I learned a life lesson I believe more people should learn.

I now see luck in a different light. I had thought of it as something most desirable that might happen to me. I have learned that, for one to attract good luck to oneself, it is necessary to take advantage of opportunities and to work hard. I also believe that for one to attract good fortune (good luck), one must give good fortune to others. In particular, you get a blessing or good fortune by being a blessing to others in that, by helping others who cannot repay you, you set in motion the opportunities for others to help you that you cannot repay.

Step Five

Clarify the issue(s) of unforgiveness. A person can't fix a problem if he doesn't know what the problem is. That is also the way with unforgiveness: you cannot truly forgive if you don't know what you need to forgive the person. It is hard for some to understand that they have unforgiveness toward God or the deceased.

An example is a mother and her twenty-four-year-old daughter; they had become very close five years earlier during the death and grieving period of the mother's husband and the girl's father. The two did almost everything together. The daughter's decision to move out was a big shock for the mother, but the mother said that she understood her daughter's decision. However, inwardly she felt rejected, associating it with the rejection she felt at her husband's death.

The mother began to act out in passive-aggressive ways (doing things to hurt her daughter's feelings). The daughter, picking up on the mother's attitude toward her, began to show her anger toward her mother. The mother wanted to forgive the daughter for her angry actions but kept feeling the hurt because she did not recognize her feelings of rejection.

The problem as I see it is that the mother was dealing with forgiving the symptoms of the disease but not the disease itself. The daughter's angry actions were the symptom; the rejection she was feeling was the disease itself. Before dealing with the hurtful reactions, the mother needed to forgive the father for the rejection she felt, forgive God for taking the father away, and then forgive the daughter for the hurt feelings created by her leaving. Forgiveness has to be direct, not indirect.

In counseling families going through grief and loss, I have witnessed many times where people blow up over the smallest conflict. One example I heard was when a distant relative took a flower at a funeral, which is the custom of remembering the deceased for many people. One of the immediate family members went into rage over the act. One can clearly see that her anger was not simply because someone took a flower. It is hard for some people to understand that they have unforgiveness toward the deceased for leaving them or toward God for taking the deceased away. You cannot fix a problem if you don't know what the problem is. Clarifying the issue of forgiveness is an important step in working through painful situations.

Drug addicts in denial will never deal with their drug problem; they blame other things for the problems drugs created. People who sabotage their lives who are motivated by past hurts will often blame other people or things for the problems they have created. Clarifying the issues of hurts and unforgiveness is clarifying the motive behind our actions. Are our actions motivated by love and forgiveness or hate and hurts?

The two hardest issues to clarify are death and divorce. People have described divorce as dealing with the death of a loved one that you have to talk to from time to time. Many report that they seem to be overwhelmed with conflicting emotions. It is hard to clarify how one feels. One must first focus on forgiving oneself and then the issues from the former lover.

Step Six

If possible, try to be empathetic with the person or situation that caused the issue(s) of unforgiveness and/or reframe the past. What helps people treat past hurts with forgiveness? Psychologists who have researched what helps people forgive found that, in close, committed relationships, developing empathy for the person who hurt you makes a difference. Empathizing or being able to identify with the person who hurt you makes it easier to forgive him or her.

I once heard a preacher tell a story of a man and his two young boys who entered a city bus. The father was emotionlessly looking into space as his two sons ran up and down the aisle, jumping on the seats, knocking over passengers' bags, and making it difficult for the passengers to read their newspapers or books. After several minutes and miles on the bus, one of the passengers, being so frustrated, came up to the father and confronted him about his kids' behavior. The father shook himself as if he had been awakened from a deep sleep.

He said, "I am really sorry! We have just come from the hospital, where we found out that my wife and their mother has only a short time to live. I guess they are just burning off nervous energy."

The passengers immediately empathized with them. Before, the passengers had feelings of hatred and were ready to beat the kids; now they had feelings of compassion. Before the passengers had unforgiveness toward the kids; now they had forgiveness toward them. The passengers empathized with the kids and their father, which led them to forgiveness. Put yourself in the other person's shoes.

Empathize. Consider what was going on in the person's life when he or she hurt you. As an example of empathy, imagine you are driving down a highway when a speeding car cuts you off, almost forcing you off the road as he speeds by. At the time it happens, you may feel so angry you think about trying to catch him and giving him a piece of your mind. When you get home, you see on the news that the driver of that car is a father who was racing home to save his daughter from a burning, locked building, to which only he had the key.

A person's perspective of another person changes with understanding the meaning behind the actions. Think about a time when someone hurt you; maybe someone cut you off on the road. Think for a minute; if you had an emergency, wouldn't you speed and cut off people too? When we try to think of a reason why we would do the same thing if we were in the same position, it minimizes the incident. I know I have done some wrong things without knowing.

Is there anyone who can say that he or she has not done something wrong (hurt people) out of ignorance? Even the people who crucified Jesus believed they were doing the right thing! The best example of empathy is Jesus' death on the cross: "Father, forgive them; for they know not what they do" (people crucified Jesus out of ignorance—Luke 23:34). If you can put yourself in the shoes of the person who hurt you and think of a reason why you would do the same, it makes it easier to forgive him or her. There is a flipside to empathy, however. In cases of rape and child abuse, it is unhealthy to empathize with the abuser. (Justifying abuse perpetuates the abuse.) I have worked with survivors who have found some good that came out of a totally bad situation. They have learned to reframe the pain of the past.

Reframing

Sometimes events in life, like rape and child abuse, are so painful that we have to reframe our thinking and attitudes about the events. Reframing sometimes helps us to look at the past differently. We cannot do anything to change the events of our lives, but we can change our attitude about them or the way we see them.

I once heard a preacher use a quote from Dr. Charles Swindoll:

> Attitude is more important than facts. It is more important than the past, than education, than money, than circumstances, than failures, than successes, than what other people think or say or do. It is more important than appearance, giftedness or skill. It will make or break a company...a church...a home. The remarkable thing is we have a choice every day regarding the attitude we will embrace for that day. We cannot change our past...we cannot change the fact that people will act in a certain way. We cannot change the inevitable. The only thing we can do is play on the one string we have, and that is our attitude...I am convinced that life is 10% what happens to me and 90% how I react to it. And so it is with you...we are in charge of our attitude.

When one reframes, one is changing one's attitude about the event.

An example of reframing occurred when I worked in an alternative school summer program. The school helped over-aged middle-school students transition into high schools. I was asked to counsel a young man who had anger-control issues with his only female teacher. The student did not have problems with his male teachers. Our sessions focused on his anger toward his mother.

I asked, "Fifteen years from now, when you are rich and famous, can you forgive her then?"

He said, "I will never forgive her for the stuff she did. You don't know all the stuff she did."

As he worked through the steps of forgiveness, he continued to become stuck. Each time he imagined his mother and the painful events of

34

the past, his anger returned. He began to reframe his attitude about what had happened, understanding that it had made him closer to, and more protective of, his brothers, thereby bringing them all closer. He reframed his thinking about those events, thereby reframing his feelings about those events.

The best example of reframing is in the Bible. After Joseph's brothers wanted to kill him but then threw him into a dry well and sold him into slavery, he forgave them in Genesis 50:15–21:

> And when Joseph's brethren saw that their father was dead, they said, Joseph will peradventure hate us, and will certainly requite us all the evil which we did unto him. And they sent a messenger unto Joseph, saying, Thy father did command before he died, saying, so shall ye say unto Joseph, Forgive, I pray thee now, the trespass of thy brethren, and their sin; for they did unto thee evil: and now, we pray thee, forgive the trespass of the servants of the God of thy father. And Joseph wept when they spake unto him. And his brethren also went and fell down before his face; and they said, Behold, we be thy servants. And Joseph said unto them, Fear not: for am I in the place of God? But as for you, ye thought evil against me; but God meant it unto good, to bring to pass, as it is this day, to save much people alive. Now therefore fear ye not: I will nourish you, and your little ones. And he comforted them, and spake kindly unto them."

Joseph reframed the pain of the past seeing it in the light of the present. The suffering in his past created the triumph of his present and his future!

Step Seven

Pray for the person or situation toward which you have unforgiveness. Prayer at its foundation is expressing a desire to God. When I talk about prayer in this book, I mean verbally expressing a desire. The confessional prayer I ask my clients to repeat when they have those angry or hurt feelings is, "Father, I forgive (name of the person or situation), and I release him or her to go on to greater good. Father, I forgive (name of the person or situation), and I release myself to go on to greater good." I ask clients to repeat this prayer daily with the same intensity of the hurt feelings and as often as they have those feelings. By praying for the release of others, you release yourself! By verbally expressing a desire for something good to happen to someone who has hurt you, you release good in your own life. For many of my clients, it is a powerful, freeing experience.

Prayer is one of the most powerful tools one can use to forgive. I've learned to forgive through prayer. In my first working experience as a drug counselor in a large metropolitan school district, I worked in two schools—the smaller school two days a week and the larger school three days a week. The smaller school had more troubled students. I saw that the smaller school needed more attention, and I, wanting to do a good job, would often spend my lunchtime eating with the students at the smaller school. For months I noticed that the principal of the smaller school would not speak to me and only grunted when I spoke to her. She would mumble to herself under her breath (of her anger toward someone). At first I did not know who she was talking about. For weeks I tried to figure out why she was mad at me. I made an appointment with her secretary to meet with the principal so we could talk about programming events for the upcoming school year.

We met, and I talked about the things I had been doing at the school, and the plans I had about school programming for the upcoming year. The meeting seemed to be going well, and then I asked how she felt about my performance at the school. She began to accuse me of disturbing the school and spying on her. Apparently someone in the school was informing her supervisor about things going on in the school. I had no idea there were problems at the school and even less of an idea of who to tell if I did see a problem. As she accused me of sabotaging what she was trying to do, all I could do was to sit there and say, "No, Miss, I didn't do that," or "No, Miss, I did not say that." The more I denied things, the more she seemed to insist that I did. She said that I would not be working at her school, and if she had her way, I would never work with students again!

I came away from the meeting feeling confused, and soon my confusion turned to anger. I said to myself, "How dare she accuse me of spying on her? How could she believe I would do such a thing? Why is she trying to destroy me when I was only trying to help her by spending extra time with the kids?" I was really hurt and angry because of the accusations. Angrily speaking against her caused my angry feelings to grow. Matthew 15:11 says, "Not that which goeth into the mouth defileth [or corrupts] a man; but that which cometh out of the mouth, this defileth a man." I could not believe this was happening to me. I could not sleep. I began to stuff my feelings by eating, but the angry feelings grew greater and greater. (I was sabotaging my health.)

Being a young man at the time, I got most of my identity and self-worth from my job. I could not think straight. I began to seek God for an answer to my problem. The answer came—pray for her! At first my prayers for her were selfish: "Lord, save that crazy lady!" That seemed to intensify my anger. Again I sought God and God said to pray for her to have the best in her life, just as I prayed that I might have the best for my life! I began to pray, "Lord, bless her!" In time, I prayed, "God, give her your best!" I started to begin to be able to think about the principal without having feelings of resentment and hurt. I started seeing success in overcoming those ill feelings and was encouraged to pray harder for her. I later could think about her and have joy and happiness toward her, not hate and anger. Now I can truly say I really want her to have the best God has for her!

This event (learning to forgive) has proven to be one of the most pivotal learning experiences in my life. I have since had more hurtful things happen to me, but without that experience of learning to forgive, I can't see how I would have been able to go through those later, greater hurts. I would not be where I am today. I believe that unforgiveness would have held me back from becoming the person I am today.

Through this, I have learned to face hate with love. With the help of God, through prayer, one can live up to this commandment: "Bless them which persecute you: bless, and curse not… Recompense to no man evil for evil" (Rom. 12:14, 17). Praying is the act of making your desire known. The act of desiring good for someone helps to create pleasant feelings for that person. Praying for the good for someone who has hurt you releases God to bring good things to you.

I remind my reader about the story of Job in that God was angry with Job's friends because they were falsely accusing him of wrongdoing in Job 42:10, which says, "And the Lord turned the captivity of Job, when he prayed for his friends: also the Lord gave Job twice as much as he had before."

When you pray for someone to get the best and God starts to give him or her the best, be happy for that person. If your hurt feelings return, go back to step three!

Step Eight

Affirmations of forgiveness are a way of detoxifying one's thoughts and negative self-talk. This allows you to catch these thoughts and challenge them rather than simply being enraged or hurt by them. Luke 6:28 says, "Bless them that curse you, and pray for them which despitefully use you." The word *blesses* means to speak well of. Speaking well of the person who hurt you, or the one you have unforgiveness for, is in fact affirming forgiveness. Matthew 15:11 says, "Not that which goeth into the mouth defileth a man; but that which cometh out of the mouth, this defileth a man." What comes out of our mouths affects our hearts or how we feel. The "defiling (or corrupting) of a man" is defiling or the corrupting of one's thoughts, heart, or feelings. We can speak blessings that heal or poisons that kill. Proverbs 18:21 says, "Death and life are in the power of the tongue: and they that love it shall eat the fruit." Remember Proverbs 4:23: "Keep thy heart with all diligence; for out of it are the issues of life." How people feel affects what comes out of their mouths, and what comes out of their mouths reinforces how they feel. This oftentimes creates a growing cycle in one's life.

What one says affects how one feels, and how one feels affects what one says. One's hurt feelings cause one to speak more hurts, and speaking more hurts causes the hurt to grow. This cycle goes around and around getting faster like water going down a drain. Luke 6:45 says it this way: "A good man out of the good treasure of his heart bringeth forth that which is good; and an evil man out of the evil treasure of his heart bringeth forth that which is evil: for of the abundance of the heart his mouth speaketh." People who speak cursing bring forth more cursed situations, and people who speak blessing bring forth more blessed situations. New-age psychology has recognized the power of affirmations; that is why you can find so many positive affirmation or self-talk tapes and compact discs in bookstores. They have found that if you speak positively, then positive things happen, but if you speak negatively, negative things happen. If you speak life into a situation, there will be life in that situation. If you speak death into a situation, you will have death in that situation.

I once heard, in a sexual addiction seminar, "If sex addicts do not control their thoughts, their thoughts will control them," thereby leading a person deeper into his sexual addiction. I believe the same is true for all of life's problems. If we don't control the thoughts and feelings about a problem, the thoughts and feelings about that problem will control us (anxiety disorder).

The affirmations of forgiveness are ways of challenging and changing those thoughts and feelings. Studies have found that the more frequently respondents thought about revenge or forgiveness, the more likely they were to act upon these thoughts.

Here are some examples of negative thoughts:

- I hate him/her!
- He/she makes me sick!
- I'll make them pay!
- I will get them back!
- They'd better watch their backs!
- I wish they were dead!
- I hope I get a chance to get them back!
- I wish something bad would happen to them!
- They're mine!
- I want to see them get what they deserve!
- They're scum!
- I can't tolerate thinking about that person!
- I'm going to get even!
- I want to see them hurt and miserable!

The first affirmations of forgiveness are similar to the prayer of forgiveness: *"I forgive all those who have emotionally hurt or offended me, and I release them to go on to greater good. I forgive all those who have emotionally hurt or offended me, and I release myself to go on to greater good."* I ask clients to repeat this affirmation daily with the same intensity of the hurt feelings and as often as they have those feelings.

Sometimes people have long forgotten or covered up the past hurts, but their behaviors are continually driven by those past hurts. In that case, the person must look at the other self-defeating, self-sabotaging behavior and repeat the above affirmation.

In the Song of Solomon, he tells us, "It is the little foxes that destroy the grape vine, not the big foxes. It is the little sins that destroy us, not the big ones." So too are the little, unresolved frustrations that keep us enslaved.

We can readily see how great trauma like rape, murder, and other abuses can affect a person's actions and behaviors but not recognize the accumulated effect of past hurts or accumulated hurts. Thus the affirmations are used to overcome past hurts.

Other Forgiveness Affirmations
- I want them to have the best.
- I want to give them a new start and renew the relationship!

- I want to be friendlier and show concern for them!
- I accept them!
- I am thinking about how to make amends!
- I love myself enough to release them!
- He/she deserves the best!
- God please give them the best!

The more positive emotion you put into the affirmation, the more effective it is on one's unconscious and unforgiveness. It is similar to encouraging a child at a sporting event; the harder you yell to encourage a child, the more the child will believe it is true, and the harder he/she will work to make that encouragement come true. People may have had in their childhood long-forgotten hurts and resentments that affect the way they interact with others today. Those past hurts and resentments lay the foundation for how well we get along with others. We can establish a new foundation with affirmation.

Jesus said that the kingdom of God is like a person planting seeds. We have to realize that Satan is trying to build a kingdom as well. Earlier I talked about how a father's angry words affected his kids. I have seen that happen both locally and globally. I have seen where one police officer's racial actions make whole cities hate all police. I have seen parents angrily speaking about one white teacher, causing their children to distrust all teachers, which makes it hard for them to learn. I have seen people all over the world begin to treat Muslims differently because of the actions of a few Muslims on 9/11.

Most young people become racists not because of their experiences. They become racists because of other people's experiences (or the words spoken to them).

Many people say that today's youths don't show respect to others. It seems as if the harder one tries to force a young person to be respectful, the more disrespectful the person becomes. When one tries to reshape a young person's foundation of respect, it tends to reinforce the initial belief that established that foundation. The affirmations help to establish for a person a new foundation. *If we want to change the way we think and feel, we need to change what we say!* The forgiveness affirmations can not only affect the person but also affect those around that person, thereby affecting the world. What a person says affects the mood of the people around him or her. The words affect the atmosphere. The collective individual atmospheres affect the communities.

The collective individual communities affect the nation. The collective individual nations affect our world. Forgiveness can change the world we live in! It starts with us and spreads outward! I will talk more about the atmosphere in step twelve.

Families with Forgiveness

I am often asked to speak in marriage conferences and seminars on forgiveness or asked to conduct marital or premarital counseling. The key to a healthy marriage is forgiveness! There are no two people who will agree 100 percent of the time; even identical twins disagree from time to time. How can you expect two different people to agree 100 percent of the time? The problems come when we are hurt behind those disagreements. For whatever reason, we sometimes take things personally and get offended by the person being so totally different than ourselves. The truth of the matter is if you were exactly the same, one of you would not be needed. Your differences are there to bring balance to both of your lives. I know it is frustrating for you to overcome the seemingly crazy opinions your spouse has about things.

Remember Webster defines forgiveness this way: "To cease to feel resentment against on the account of wrong committed." But sometimes no wrongs were truly committed for resentment to be felt. Sometimes resentment may build up from some of the smallest disagreements. I have seen where small things become big things because of what one or both of the partners say about it. Death and life are in the power of the tongue. And I can tell you some stories of how one spouse's words killed the marriage! With divorces in the church at over 50 percent, God's Word is really true: "If any man among you seems to be religious and bridle not his tongue, but deceive his own heart, this man's religion is in vain" (James 1:26).

I talked about blaming earlier. The words we speak in blaming our spouse are rooted in unforgiveness. We have to learn to move beyond the hurt and resentment. People who are hurting, hurt people; many times you hurt the ones closest to you. The one we love the most in most cases is our spouses. By speaking words of blame to our spouses, we give away our power to change things. We can't do anything about it because they are the ones who caused it; they have to fix it! You may ask, what if it is truly your partner's fault? If you never made a mistake, then you can cast the first stone; if not, do as the people did. As Jesus said, you without sin cast the first stone. The people dropped their stones and moved on. Forgive him or her. Drop it and move on.

I have found that many of the problems couples face come from hurts or baggage from past relationships. People make their spouses pay the penalty for the hurts others have caused. Even seemingly great past relationships overflow into present relationships. One's interactions in past relationships lead to expectations in present relationships. This is obvious in people coming from abuse, who flinch when their spouses get angry. Also, people are overly suspicious about spousal betrayal when they've experienced betrayal in the past. But good qualities and moments in your past relationships can also impact your current one in a negative way. For example, when you remember things like your first date, first kiss, and other firsts with your former mate, you often hold your current spouse to the same standard. Simply put, the actions your other mate performed may not be important to your present spouse. In short, one's past relationships set up the present relationship for failure if you continue to dwell on it. I know it sounds kind of crazy to forgive our former partners for good things they did, but drop it and move on. This frees you to receive the good qualities your current spouse has to offer.

While helping couples work through seemingly small problems, I have found that couples allow hurts to fester and spill over into other areas of their lives. The hurts affect the way they talk to one another. After a time of talking to one another from an attitude of hurt and anger, they began to build up more and more resentment toward each other. Marriages, like tires, go flat more from slow leaks than blowouts. Fewer couples get divorces from one big problem; often couples divorce because of multiple smaller problems. If one does not fix one's slowly leaking tire, it will eventually go flat. Similarly, if we don't fix/forgive the problems of our marriages, they too will go flat. The sooner we fix the slowly leaking tire, the sooner we will ride smoother. In the same way, the sooner we fix the small problems of our marriages through forgiveness, the sooner our marriages will ride smoother. As forgiveness can smooth out your marriage, so to can forgiveness smooth out your lives! *Think about it!*

I have found while working with teens in school that their seemingly crazy actions or behaviors are products of their dysfunctional relationship with their parent(s). Looking at my own life, most of my own crazy behaviors are products of my initial relationship with my father. Although I have painfully worked through my father issues, I realize that is why I had a difficult time forgiving people, especially males in authority. That's why I feel it is so important for us to speak the affirmation of forgiveness: *"I forgive all those who have emotionally hurt or offended me and I release them to go on to greater good. I forgive all those who have emotionally hurt or offended me and I release myself to go on to greater good."*

Fifty percent of all marriages in the America end in divorce. The divorce rate in America for second marriage is 60 percent. The divorce rate in America for third marriage is 73 percent. That statistic speaks volumes about our problem with forgiving one another. If a person has a hard time forgiving a partner the first time in marriage, it will be even harder the second time around and even more difficult the third time. When you walk in unforgiveness, it becomes easier and easier to walk in unforgiveness. When one learns to walk in forgiveness, it becomes easier and easier to walk in forgiveness. When the Bible talks about walking in sin or the ways of God, it is talking about practicing sin or God's ways. The more one practices sin, the easier that sin gets. Also, the more a person practices God's will (forgiveness), the easier it is to do God's will (forgiveness). How do we know if we forgive someone?

Step Nine

Take a forgiveness inventory. Imagine the person or situation in your mind who hurt you and toward which you have unforgiveness for twenty seconds.
a) If you have feelings of happiness and/or best wishes for the person or situation, go on to step ten.
b) If you have feelings of pain, hurt, or resentment, then go back to step three.

For some people, it is not an individual they need to forgive but a consequence of events that led to hurt feelings. In that case, we need to forgive that situation(s). I have had clients who have become homeless because of a fire. They stayed homeless because they could not move beyond that situation (the fire). Every time I talked to them about their lives or their futures, they would continue to say, "If only we did not have that fire!"

I have had clients who have said that they have forgiven people in their lives, but their behavior toward the people who hurt them is passive aggressive. Their behaviors seemed to indicate that they have unforgiveness toward that person, but when they look closely at how they feel about the person, they see their unforgiveness. If you think about the person for twenty seconds and still have hurt feelings, you need to continue working on forgiveness. The test of forgiveness is the same as the test of love: wanting the best for someone. The clearest picture of forgiveness is Jesus wanting the best (eternal life) for those who crucified him: "Father, forgive them for they know not what they do." Also consider Hebrews 12:2: "Jesus…for the joy that was set before him endured the cross." When we look beyond the hurt of the now, we gain the self-control of the future. If you do not allow yourself to be dragged back to the self-sabotaging behaviors of unforgiveness, go on to step ten.

If you can imagine or think about the person or situation in your mind for twenty seconds without having hurt feelings or feelings of resentment, it is a sure sign that you have forgiven that person. Forgiveness is the release of all the negative emotions associated with that person. If you can visualize or hold the image of that person or situation in your mind and want the best for him or her, you clearly have forgiven that person. If to err is human, and to forgive is divine, then your life is divinely inspired. If you continue to have hurt feelings toward that individual or situation, then you should go back to step three.

If you find yourself having thoughts or doing things that could hurt the person toward whom you have unforgiveness, continue to ask God to help you to forgive. Matthew 7:7 says, "He that [continues to] knock, the door will be open." It is important to note that one's unconsciousness can, many times, sabotage one's life if forgiveness is not obtained and continued. These steps should be seen as a continuous process to forgiveness. It is not a one-time shot, or "One, two, and I'm through." Some people, when they have forgiven a person for hurting them, have difficulty re-forgiving that person. I have counseled with couples who wanted to get a divorce because one squeezed the toothpaste from the middle or did not replace tissue in the bathroom. It is accumulated hurts, but it is also the straw that broke the camel's back. Events in life come up that reopen the wound that forgiveness had closed up. A person must be willing to rework the first steps that led him/her to the achievement of forgiveness. Some people can forgive others but not themselves. Why is it important to forgive oneself? Because people can be trapped in the cycle of emotional addiction—using drugs, for example.

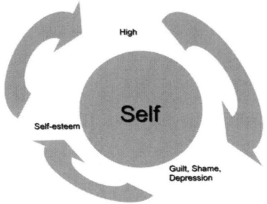

One uses drugs to feel good, but for every high, there is a corresponding low. At first the low may be a blah feeling, but later one recognizes the feeling as guilt, shame, and depression, which affects the way one feels about oneself. This then gives one more reasons to go get high, and the cycle goes around and around, getting faster like water going down a drain. You can substitute drugs with sex, gambling, or other addictions; the result is the same. No one is perfect. We all make mistakes. Guilt, like past hurts, drives us to self-sabotaging behaviors. Forgiveness frees one from self-sabotaging behaviors. I once worked with a minister with a sexual addiction. His guilt made him feel empty inside. He often filled the emptiness with sexual gratification. His guilt was driving his addiction. Once the minister learned to walk in forgiveness, he learned to walk in freedom.

Step Ten

Be ready to forgive as issues and situations come up. Again, these steps are a continuous process. One of the most powerful tools for deliverance is unconditional love. I have seen unconditional love and forgiveness heal and work a miracle in people's lives. Walking in forgiveness is practicing on every opportunity. I am not saying that you are to allow others to walk over you, but in conducting conflict mediations, I tell people, "The greater the distrust, the clearer the boundaries must be." There are some people who you will see day in and day out who will continue to hurt you. You can love people without allowing them to cross any boundaries.

One example was when a young man kept seeing his brother continuing to hurt their mother. Because of the brother's drug addiction, he would steal things or money from their mother. Every time he saw his brother, his anger returned. He had to continue to pray and say forgiveness affirmations for his brother so his anger would not return. He continued to pray that his unconditional love would lead his brother to Christ.

There Is a Purpose behind Our Pain
In working with young adults, I have found the biggest question that stops people from moving beyond the painful issues is, why? They question God! I believe *God allows pain to increase your greatness* (Ps. 71:21)!

As I discussed before, I have come to understand that there really is a divine design to every experience. No matter how painful, every experience is a reflection of something we need to know about ourselves. There is a purpose behind our pain. Hebrews 12:2 says, "Jesus…for the joy that was set before him endured the cross." Also Romans 8:28 says, "And we know that God causes everything to work together for the *good* of those who love God…"

As a drug counselor, in the past I questioned why some people have greater struggles than others, why some were instantly healed through deliverance from drugs but others were healed through disciplining themselves. Some people were healed and walked after an injury through a miraculous deliverance while others struggled and learned to walk again after an injury from disciplining themselves.

The answer I believe I have found is that God wants to develop more *character* in some people that they will need later for leadership. A preacher once told me a vivid story of how he developed character during his difficulties while going through basic training, and later of his survival in the jungle doing guerrilla warfare. While he was going through basic training, he felt like they pushed him, as well as others, too hard. He felt like they were stressing and exhausting him for no reason, but the things that he hated doing were the things that kept him alive in the jungle. I see the struggles that he endured during his basic training prepared him for his survival and later success in life. God caused those things to work for his good! He told a story of a shelling (bombing) in the jungle where he ran to the place where the bomb had just exploded. He believed that if a bomb exploded, there it would be a long time before another bomb hit in that area again. He saw people run into an explosion trying to escape from an explosion. Often we run into an explosion trying to run from an explosion. I have seen people running into hurt trying to run from hurt.

Young people used a term to describe people going from one stupid situation to the next stupid situation. They call it "stuck on stupid." Their hurts of the past are motivating their stupid behaviors. We, not like the pastor, don't like to face the destruction and find safety where the bomb recently exploded. Likewise, we don't like to face the hurt others have caused in our lives. I have seen people running from hurts run into hurts. I believe they would stop running into hurts if they would only stop and face the hurts. Forgiveness! Romans 5:3–5 reads, "Knowing that tribulation [suffering] produces perseverance, and perseverance, *character*, and character, hope. Now hope [positive expectations] does not disappoint..." (NKJV).

We too can endure the painful experiences to enjoy the strength in character we gain through those experiences. I define character as "inner strength." I believe this is one of the purposes behind our pain. A way to reframe our hurts for Christians is to realize that there is a purpose behind our pain. I believe David reframed his pain. Psalm 71:20–21 reads, "Thou which has shown me great and sore troubles shalt quicken me again and shalt bring me up again from the depth of the earth. *Thou shalt increase my greatness*, and comfort me on every side" (KJV). *I believe God wants to increase your greatness!* I have counseled a young man who was angry with God because of the pain he endured, but the pain developed the character or charisma to lead other young men out of a life of gangs and violence. I have counseled a young lady who was raised by her grandmother. She too was angry with God at the death of her grandmother. Because of her pain, she began working with ladies who were making bad choices in their lives, but because of her charisma, she was able to help those young ladies make better choices.

I see a very close similarity between the children of Israel who didn't get into the Promised Land and Christians today. That similarity is the complaining. First Corinthians 10:9–10 reads, "Neither let us tempt Christ, as some of them also tempted, and were destroyed of serpents. Neither murmur ye, as some of them also murmured, and were destroyed of the destroyer."

I believe murmuring/blaming and complaining opens the doors in our lives for the enemy to come in, just like murmuring/blaming and complaining kept the children of Israel from the promises and blessings of

God. We too can miss out on God's promises and blessings when we murmur and complain. *When we complain, we are praising the problem.* But I like to be like King David, "A man after God's heart," who always talked about waiting or trusting in the Lord. David talked about his problems in the Psalms but always turned it into praise. Psalm 42:5 reads, "Why art thou cast down, O my soul? And why art thou disquieted in me? Hope [positive expectations] thou in God: for I shall yet praise him..." Or consider Job, who said, "Though he slay me, yet will I trust in him" (Job 13:15). Complaining or murmuring about our situation is the polar opposite of trusting God. David said, "It is good for me that I have been afflicted..." (Ps. 119:71).

I do not mean that we cannot share our hurts and problems with other Christian brothers and sisters, for Galatians 6:2 says, "Bear ye one another's burdens, and so fulfill the law of Christ." No, what I'm talking about is complaining about the problem and giving power to that problem, thereby nullifying the power of God. Our words are seeds that will grow in our hearts!

What seeds are you planting? Talking about the hurtful issue strengthens the hurt feelings about the issue. We begin to trust in what we see and feel more than trusting in God!

One of the more powerful revelations God gave to me was when He reminded me of a past conflict mediation. There were two girls in conflict about someone spreading a secret. One girl reported that she only told two people about the secret, and it had to be the girl she was in conflict with who shared her secret. Once I heard that it could have been someone else who could have told her secret, I began to explain that it could have been the other girl who shared her secret. The other girl said that she didn't tell anyone. She said, "Oh no I know it wasn't her that told." I began to push and push the other girl theory. She said, "I've known her for years...she knows worse secrets about me... If she wanted to share something, she could have shared a lot worse... In the past I have hurt her and given her reasons to get back at me by sharing one or more of my secrets, but she didn't!" No matter what I said, I could not shake her from her trust in her friend. She had an unshakable faith in her friend!

God asked me why I couldn't have that same kind of faith toward Him. He then reminded me of Hebrews 11:6: "But without faith it is impossible to please Him: for he that cometh to God must believe that he is, and that he is a rewarder of them that diligently seek him." That is the kind of character that God wants! Just like friends learn to trust one another, we have to learn to trust God. Thus God gives us experiences of struggles and pains where we learn to trust Him. Our trust in God grows when we obey Him by forgiving those who hurt us.

Another purpose behind our pain is to help others. Second Corinthians 1:4 says, "Who comforteth us in all our tribulation, that we may be able to comfort them which are in any trouble, by the comfort wherewith we ourselves are comforted of God."

We are God's representatives here on earth; we are to show or represent God's love and forgiveness to others. Jesus taught us to "Pray Thy kingdom come thy will be done..." God's will is for us to have love and forgiveness for one another. We can create an atmosphere of love and forgiveness or allow the enemy to create an atmosphere of hurts and counter-hurts where hurting people hurt others, which eventually creates an atmosphere of crime and violence. This is why I believe that our character is so important to God. Romans 8:28 says, "And we know that *God causes everything to work together for the good* of those who love God and are called according to his purpose for them."

If we look at the heroes of the Bible, we see godly men and women going through struggles and coming out stronger. Previously I talked about Joseph the dreamer, his struggles of life, and how he forgave. David also showed forgiveness when he had opportunity to get revenge on Saul but, "David said to Abishai, Destroy him not: for who can stretch forth his hand against the Lord's anointed" (1 Sam. 26:9). In my lifetime, I have had examples of walking in forgiveness and becoming stronger.

One of the closest examples of forgiveness is my mother. When I was young, I did some things that really hurt her, but she kept on loving me. At the time it happened, I thought to myself, *If I had a kid who did the same thing to me I would kill him or her!* I learned by her example; I saw true forgiveness!

The second is Dr. Martin Luther King Jr., who I believe was one of the most charismatic people of the twentieth century. I believe his charisma was developed by going through the struggles. *God causes those things to work for our good!* People are not born with charisma; it is developed through life's difficulties. People are drawn to people with charisma. Dr. King's charisma helped to lead people to lay their lives on the line by demonstrating during the fight for civil rights. Who knows—the pain that you are going through or have gone through may give you the drawing power that leads someone to Christ.

Many of the most charismatic people on television today have a story of pains and hurts before becoming famous. I believe it was those hurts and pains that created the charisma in their lives. People living on the streets or in prison have similar stories, but their outcomes are polar opposites. You can allow your hurts to make you or break you! This is the reason we need to forgive. Pain sometimes comes to show us ourselves. Pain reveals what is truly in our hearts. I have found that pain reveals what is in my heart. If I stomp my toe and curse words come out my mouth, the pain did not put the curse words in. It only showed me what was in my heart from the start. Pain reveals one's true character.

The question people without character often ask is, "Is it safe to walk in forgiveness in today's world?" With all the violence and crime today—

child molestations, domestic violence, drive-by shootings, gangs and hate groups—violence is all we hear about. Not to mention the war on terrorism: should we forgive them and let these persons go unpunished?

Being ready and willing to forgive does not mean that we allow people to be unaccountable for their actions. Forgiveness suggests that people seek fairness by holding offenders accountable for their actions. I can forgive someone for shooting me with a gun, but just because I forgave him doesn't mean I should give him a gun so he can shoot me again or worse, shoot someone else. Just because you forgive someone doesn't mean that you have changed your name to Matt—short for doormat—in that people can walk all over you! You will have to forgive the person who sold you a lemon of a car, but you don't have to trust him or her and continue buying cars from him or her.

Once I counseled a wife of an abusive husband. The wife read my book and said, "I have to forgive him when he apologizes." She explained that her husband told her that he only hit her because she made him mad and that he wouldn't hit her if she didn't make him mad! I told her that he did not apologize for hitting her; he justified why he hit her. I also told her that *any sin we can justify we will repeat* because we made it okay to continue doing it by justifying it. We must pray for others but not be preyed upon by others. Can you imagine a world without consequences? Imagine a world where people can do anything regardless of the hurt or harm it causes to others.

During the question-and-answer time when I speak at conferences, I am often asked about divorce from a physically abusive mate. Can a person divorce because of abuse? I have seen God lead people to stay in an abusive marriage, which led the mate to Christ. I also have seen God release people through divorce. I believe we should be dogmatic about what the Bible is dogmatic about and not dogmatic about the things the Bible is not dogmatic about. The Bible only makes allowances for unfaithfulness. Matthew 19:6 says, "What therefore God hath joined together, let not man put asunder." But the Bible also talks about how we are to be good stewards of everything God has given us, including our bodies and their safety.

If the scripture does not give clear directions, we must seek God's direction in the matter. We have to be led by the Spirit. I encourage people to give the situation the test of love. All our actions should be motivated by love. Am I divorcing him/her because of hurt and anger or because I need to protect what God has invested in you? I also encourage them to seek counsel from their pastor, their spiritual covering. His or her job is to lead you in the right direction. I encourage people to spend time with God, listening for His direction. Pain reveals one's true character!

I'd like to again emphasize the fact that it takes courage and strength to forgive. Someone may knock you down, but unforgiveness keeps you down. Forgiveness, on the other hand, stands you back up. When you acknowledge that you have been victimized, you break the chains of psychological slavery.

I have also seen where receiving forgiveness helps people become free from psychological slavery. I always tell people, "Hurting people hurt people!" I know of a married couple where, because the wife was abused by her father as a child, she subconsciously did things to hurt her husband. Her unforgiveness of her father was sabotaging her relationship with her husband. Although she regretted hurting her husband, she continued to find herself hurting him over and over again. She was using her husband to unconsciously get back at her father. The husband, because he knew of the childhood abuse, responded by representing her heavenly Father with unconditional love. Through his act of unconditional love, she learned to forgive her father, which resulted in healing in her life.

When one continues to walk in forgiveness, it frees one from the emotional bondage that holds others back. Step ten is being ready to forgive as different issues and situations come up. Be ready and willing to continue in the freedom that forgiveness gave you. No longer allow yourself to become entangled in the bondage of unforgiveness.

Step Eleven

Continue to take inventory. Once you have been set free, why should you allow yourself to fall back into bondage? I like to answer that question by using a saying that young people in the past used when someone was challenging them to fight: "You'd better check yourself before you wreck yourself!" My belief is that we need to check all of our negative responses to emotions before they wreck our lives ("guard your heart"). We should do as the Bible says in 1 Corinthians 11:28, 31: "But let a man examine himself...For if we would judge ourselves, we should not be judged."

In group counseling for youth on probation, I ask the following questions: Who is the only person who can stop you from becoming successful? What are the emotions that hinder a person's progress to success? What are the emotions that stop a person's progress to success? Why do smart people do crazy things? What causes people to go crazy? Have you ever held in anger and later taken it out on someone else? Are there some people who are hurting because of an absent mother or father? What will happen if a person doesn't deal with his or her past hurts? The solution to the above situations is forgiveness. While working with youth who have a lot of baggage, I've discovered it is hard for them to see their issues, but they see everyone else's issues with crystal clarity. The above questions are designed to lead them to self-examination. We all have had past hurts that affect our behavior. We have to look for the past hurts that are motivating our negative choices or behavior.

For many therapists, in self-analysis we can see the importance of examining ourselves for character defects that will hinder us from helping others. Are these my issues that are creating this transference and/or counter-transference? Or are they the client's issues?

We can imagine our lives as beautiful, green, plush gardens. We have created our gardens by placing the seeds of forgiveness and watered and fertilized them with prayers and affirmations of forgiveness. In our gardens, weeds of unforgiveness may continue to spring up. We must be vigilant to weed them out! Along with the freedom we receive through forgiveness comes the responsibility of maintaining that freedom.

The first scripture I memorized is Romans 12:2: "Be not conformed to this world, but be ye transformed by the renewing of your mind." I daily renew my mind in love and forgiveness. Continuing to take inventory is evaluating whether my actions are motivated by love and forgiveness or anger, hurt and resentment.

People who are hurting, hurt people! I remember hearing a story of a preacher dying and Jesus showing him heaven and hell. Jesus showed him hell, and the people there were in so much pain and misery. The only pleasure was in scratching, biting, and causing hurt to others who came to that place.

When I first heard that, I thought of a place full of sociopaths and psychopaths, but I remembered seeing people changed by their environment. I have seen people who, because they were bullied, started to bully others. I have seen people who, because things were taken from them, began to take things from others. I have seen caring people lose all compassion for others because of the angry, bitter environment to which they moved. People become desensitized or insensitive to the pains of others. I have worked with hardworking people who became homeless and who also became trapped in the hopeless thinking of that atmosphere. Be not conformed to this world but be ye transformed by the renewing of your mind. That is why creating a loving and forgiving environment/atmosphere is so important. "Thy kingdom come thy will be done!" We, being social beings, find it easier to adapt to our environment/atmosphere rather than change it. We have to renew our minds daily in love and forgiveness. We then can walk in a closer relationship with God and others. I will talk more about the atmosphere in step twelve.

Step Twelve

Experience a spiritual awakening, a strengthening of the relationship with God, others, and yourself, because of your walking in forgiveness. I define *spirituality* as one's relationship with oneself, others, as well as with God. For some people, it is easier to forgive others. They find it difficult to forgive God or themselves. They hold themselves prisoner to the thoughts of guilt, regret, and "what if" questions, torturing and tormenting their inner-being, reviewing the painful events in their minds over and over.

Like a child whose wound is being healed, the child scratches off the scab, opening the wound back up. Physical wounds cannot heal if we continue to fiddle with them (pulling off the scab); it is the same with emotional wounds.

Some of us make ourselves the final judges, disregarding the fact that others and God have forgiven us! If God has forgiven us, how can we make ourselves superior to God by holding ourselves in unforgiveness? God's free gift of forgiveness is yours even though you may say to yourself, "I don't deserve to be forgiven!" Sometimes we are just like the children of Israel, wandering in our personal wilderness for years because of murmurings (speaking against) and refusing to accept God's freedom and promises. Also, we can live close to God's Promised Land of freedom, but not in it! After all, God has set us free from the guilt of the past, but we are sometimes deceived into thinking we need to punish ourselves for those past mistakes.

We need to daily renew our minds in God's Word and His promises. We have to create an atmosphere of love and forgiveness in our own hearts and minds to change the atmosphere in our homes, thereby changing the atmosphere in our neighborhoods, thereby changing the atmosphere in our cities and communities, thereby changing the atmosphere in our states and nations, and finally changing the atmosphere of our world. God created mankind to have fellowship with him. To reject his forgiveness for you is to reject his relationship with you. You cannot accept God without accepting his forgiveness for you. When you reject God's forgiveness of you, you reject God. The most important relationship one has is the relationship with oneself.

One can't give what one doesn't have! One can't give love to others if one does not have it for oneself and God (or loving God in oneself). When one walks in forgiveness, one finds that the relationship with oneself is strengthened, leading to a stronger relationship with others and thereby strengthening one's relationship with God. Forgiveness involves wholeness, bringing things together, and fulfilling a sense of integrity among individuals within the organization.

Wholeness involves mending breaches, uniting fragments, and creating a sense of oneness, connection, and completion. We are spiritual beings, and we have spiritual needs. We have the need to be in good, peaceful relationship with ourselves, others, and God. I believe that is why our youths have become so violent—because we pay so little attention to the family that the spiritual needs of children are ignored (broken relationships). I believe that youths spell love "T-I-M-E"! I'm talking about quality, not quantity. You can have more of a positive effect spending five minutes telling a young man how proud you are than spending two hours in the same room watching TV.

When parents learn to forgive, children usually follow their example, which leads to wholeness and healing in the family. We gain spiritual victory in this spiritual awakening. "The weapons of our warfare are not carnal, but spiritual."

Forgiveness, a Weapon of Spiritual Warfare

As I mentioned earlier, I work in an inner-city school. I am often asked to counsel or mediate between fighting students. When I have parties of students in conflict with one another in my office, each group will report that someone from the other group is saying things about them. I have discovered that the person from each of the other groups can never be found. There is always some unseen person behind the scene evoking the conflict. We also have an unseen enemy behind the scenes motivating us to fight with one another. The Apostle Paul said, "We wrestle not with flesh and blood."

Our unseen enemy, Satan, wants us to wrestle with each other, not with him. Satan is trying to create strongholds or habits in our lives to affect the environment we live in.

Two of the biggest strongholds Satan tries to establish in our lives are anger and resentment. People who are hurting hurt other people! Unconsciously, people respond to others without realizing they are spreading anger and resentment. In spiritual warfare, the battleground is in our minds and hearts. Proverbs 4:23 reads, "Above all else, guard your heart for it is the wellspring of life" (NIV; the Hebrew word for heart means "feelings"). If Satan can win the battle for your thoughts and feelings/emotions, he has won the battle that directs your life in a negative direction.

"I have a plan for you to prosper, said the Lord" (Jer. 29:11). Satan's plan is to kill, steal and destroy (John 10:10). We cannot afford to lose this battle!

I see this battle as two kingdoms at war with each other, fighting for total control of the land. One of the kingdoms is of love and forgiveness; the other kingdom of hate and resentment. My childhood pastor, Pastor Hulan Williams, told a story that illustrates these two kingdoms.

An old Indian, an elder in his tribe, was training a young Indian in the way of wisdom. One evening, while sitting by the fire, the old Indian told the young Indian that he has two dogs constantly fighting within him, and then the older Indian retired to bed. The young Indian stayed up for hours pondering the meaning of the two dogs fighting within. It troubled him all that night. He dreamed of two dogs, imagining one red, the other blue, scratching and biting each other.

The two dogs never tired but continued to fight without stopping. As dawn broke, the young Indian could hardly restrain himself from going to wake his teacher, for he had so many questions to ask him about the two dogs. The young Indian saw his teacher coming from afar and ran to him, in his mind wondering which question to ask him first! He said to the older Indian, "I have so many questions about the two dogs fighting within you. How big are the dogs? Is there one dog that wins more than the other? What are they fighting for?" The older Indian stopped the young Indian and said, "The two dogs are my desires, one the desire to do good and the other to do evil! The one that wins the most is the one that I feed the most! How big the dog or desire gets depends on how much I feed that desire!"

We too have two desires within us, constantly fighting. The desire we feed the most is the desire we yield to, or the one that wins!

The Apostle Paul put it this way in Romans 5:16–17, "So I say live by the spirit [of God] and you will not gratify the desires of the sinful nature. For the sinful nature desires what is contrary to the Spirit, and the Spirit is contrary to the sinful nature. They are in conflict..." If we feed love and forgiveness to those thoughts and emotions, then love and forgiveness will win out in establishing our foundation, and our natural response to others will be from love and forgiveness. Also, the opposite is true if we feed anger and resentment to our thoughts and emotions. Our natural response will be from a foundation of anger and resentment. The more one feeds one's thoughts and emotions anger and resentment, the stronger that desire gets, and the more visible it becomes in one's life. This point may become clearer if you can imagine a person you know who can be described by this saying, "He or she is not prejudiced; he or she hates everyone!" This person may oppose a person or group of people, but his or her anger can quickly turn toward you or anyone else for the smallest provocation.

Changing the Atmosphere

I once heard a story about a preacher in a store where one of the store workers was very rude to him. His first thoughts were of revenge and to return bitterness for bitterness. However, he heard God say, "Bless her with some money!" After arguing with God, he relented and gave the woman the money. This in turn changed her attitude, which subsequently changed the atmosphere of the store. The environment affects every decision we make! The kingdom of God is not a place but a way of life. The people of God transform the place by creating an atmosphere of love and forgiveness.

When one feeds one's mind and heart love and forgiveness, more love and forgiveness will grow in one's life, and one will able to respond to others with more love and forgiveness. *The battle is for the control of the atmosphere.* Satan is trying to create an atmosphere of hate and anger. In some of our communities with high rates of crime and violence, he has been effective. In some of our communities with drugs, gangs, and crime, it seems as if all hope is lost. The people in these communities seem to accept, even expect violence. One might ask the question, can one person make a difference? God reminded me of when I gave my life to Jesus. There was a song that said, "I looked at my hands and they looked new. I looked at my feet and they did too!" For me, my neighborhood looked new. It did not look so depressing and hopeless. For me, God had changed the atmosphere of the neighborhood. Jesus taught us to pray, "Thy kingdom come thy will be done!" God's kingdom is a way of living that requires love and forgiveness.

I work in an inner-city school where there is a lot of violence and poverty. I have realized the spiritual battle over the atmosphere. My school, like many other schools, is test driven! Everything depends on the students' achievements on state standardized test. In order for a person to change hopeless school environments/atmospheres, administrators use the power of words. The administrators empower the teachers to believe by saying things like, "We can do it! You are doing a good job." The teachers encourage the students in the same way. The students start to say and believe that they can do it!

Truly death and life are in the power of the tongue. What a person says affects the atmosphere. There are many examples of the power of words speaking to hopeless situations, like in the book of Ezekiel. Chapter 37 talks about the valley of dry bones, but in verse 11, he explains, "Then he said unto me, Son of man, these bones are the whole house of Israel: behold, they say, Our bones are dried, and our hope is lost..." We too can and should speak to our hopeless environments and/or situations. In negative environments, we have a choice, even though it is much easier to go with the flow and not create waves, so to speak. It is much harder to swim upstream rather than going with the flow. I again remind my readers of Jesus' prayer: "Thy kingdom come thy will be done..." God is concerned about the atmosphere.

One of the clearest examples in history that shows the spiritual battle that changed the atmosphere is the Civil Rights Movement and Dr. Martin Luther King Jr. Although no man is perfect, Dr. King preached and practiced love and forgiveness. He was talked down to, spat on, beaten, and jailed, but he continued to preach and practice love and forgiveness. The fight for civil rights was won in the spiritual battle. There were two camps of thought in winning the civil rights battle. There was one camp of violence. The other camp was of nonviolence. One camp believed that if someone hit you, you should hit him or her back. If they killed one of you, then you killed one of them. If they used force to keep us out, we used force to make our way in. The two ways were the natural way of retaliation and violence and the spiritual way of nonviolence, love, and forgiveness. Civil rights were won spiritually through love, forgiveness, and a lot of prayer! I believe that we would not have the civil rights we have today if the fight had been fought in the natural arena with guns and knives.

The Word of God is our first line of defense against our enemy. Dr. Martin Luther King Jr. often quoted the Bible, "The truth shall make you free." Throughout the Bible, we can see teachings about forgiving others. I believe the truth you know is the truth you do! Truth can be seen in your actions, not in what you say! The truth that people saw on TV at that time was people being beat and killed for what they believed. That impacted the choice of which sides they wanted to be associated with. But if the fight for civil rights had been fought in the physical, natural arena, with natural guns and knives, all people would have seen were people fighting; the reason for the fight would have faded into the background. But because the protesters did not fight back, people saw the injustice of treatment and understood why they were protesting. Today we hear about wars all the time, but we soon forget the reason why they are fighting.

I believe Jesus fought spiritually, "What is easier to say, your sins are forgiven, or take up your bed and walk?" Also, when the priest and elders accused Jesus before Pilate, "He answered to him never a word, insomuch that the governor marveled greatly" (Matt. 27:11). Although he did not care for the Hebrews, he seemed to want to help Jesus, to implore Jesus to say something, but Pilate could not help Jesus if he wouldn't say something in his own defense. Jesus showed no anger toward his accusers. This caused the governor to want to free Jesus.

I recall hearing two stories of changing a KKK member or racist; one story is of a young black man, and the other was of a Jewish husband and wife. Both racist/KKK members were won over with love and forgiveness. You cannot overcome hate with hate; it only makes the hate grow stronger. We are in a spiritual battle for the souls of men and women today. I have seen the church try to use Satan's weapons of hate and unforgiveness against him. I hear church leaders say that God doesn't want the KKK or any other people to walk all over you; he wants you to fight back! We can't afford to try to win over others by using hate and unforgiveness. Once we win the spiritual battle within us through forgiveness, we can win the battles without.

While working with young people, I have learned that they believe what you do more than what you say! They don't want to hear that you have the love of Christ working in your heart. They want to see the love of Christ working in your heart. It is as if they are looking for proof that you are what you say you are! More and more today, unbelievers can find proof that people in the church are not living what they say they believe. Can we win the spiritual battle of leading them to Christ if they don't believe Christ can change their lives by loving the unlovable? The greatest spiritual awakening is the ability to love the unlovable.

Some people in hopeless situations may need to take a lesson learned from the black church experience. Historically the black church has been a place of hope for people in a hopeless environment! In the black church during slavery and the Civil Rights movement, they sang songs of hope for a better future. The congregations sang songs that changed the atmosphere of the church, which changed their outlook on the situations that they were facing.

I believe when King David was a child watching his father's sheep, he sang songs of praise to God, which created an atmosphere that gave him the courage to face the lion and the bear. I believe during the Civil Rights movement, the black church sang songs of praise to God, which created an atmosphere that gave them the courage to face the dangers of being attacked and killed.

I have learned that in those times when I'm anxious, angry, or depressed, if I sing songs of praise to God, it changes how I feel, which in turn changes my outlook on the situation I'm going through. One's perception of life is one's reality! By giving God praise, we change our outlook or perception, thereby changing our reality.

We have to change the atmosphere, or the atmosphere will change us! The New Living Translation Bible says, "Guard your heart above all else, for it determines the course of your life." First Samuel 16:7 talks about how men look at the appearance (or the outward), but God looks at the heart (the inward). Genesis 1:26 says, "And God said, Let us make man in our image…and let them have dominion…over…the earth" (KJV). God want us to have control over the atmosphere and not have the atmosphere have control over our hearts/emotions.

Growing up in a poor neighborhood, I know firsthand how an angry and hurtful environment or atmosphere can affect people's emotions, which affects their behaviors that reinforce the environment. Jesus talked about the kingdom of God. God's kingdom is that of love, peace, and forgiveness. We have to realize that Satan is trying to promote a kingdom as well. His kingdom is the outward trying to run the (heart and emotion) inward person. God's is helping people have the inner (heart and emotion) run the outward or atmosphere/environment. We must allow God to take more and more of our heart (inside) so that we can take more and more of our outside atmosphere. God works from the inside to affect the outside. Satan works from the outside to try to affect the inside or heart. Thermostats are devices that influence the temperature of the environment. Thermometers are devices that reflect the temperature of the environment. Which device best describes you?

When we talk about the anger and hurtful environment, we reinforce it! We glorify the problem thereby glorifying the author of the problem. When we glorify God, we glorify the solution to the problem. God begin working from the inside (our perceptions and feelings), thereby giving us the power to change the outside.

Conclusion

There is an old saying my pastor would often repeat when I was growing up: "It is the little foxes that destroy the grape vine, not the big foxes. It is the little sins that destroy us, not the big ones." I thought it was because he did not want us to have any fun. Now I believe that, like little foxes, little sins many times affect one's entire life. Little, unresolved frustrations keep us enslaved. In closing, I would like to remind my reader of Jesus's example of forgiveness and love—the story of the prodigal son. The father did not give his son what he deserved—to be treated as a slave. The father preferred to give him what he did not deserve. The father preferred to value relationship over fairness. As we give others what they don't deserve, God gives us what we don't deserve. In the final analysis, your forgiveness is determined by your actions, not your intentions. Our actions are decided by our conscious and unconscious thoughts and emotions. These steps direct our thoughts and emotions, thereby directing our actions and thus our lives.

If you would like to accept Jesus into your life pray this prayer out loud. "Lord Jesus I believe you died on the cross and was raised from the dead I ask you to come into my life and live your life through me. Amen

Bibliography

Anonymous. *Alcoholics Anonymous: The Big Book,* Fourth Edition. New York: Alcoholics Anonymous World Services, Inc., 2001.
Affirmations of Forgiveness
Author: Delisa King.
America (Magazine)
Jan 7, 2002. "Message for World Peace Day: No Peace Without Justice, No Justice Without Forgiveness."
Author: Pope John Paul II.
Christian Century (Magazine)
July 5, 2000. "No Future Without Forgiveness."
Author: Sarah Ruben.
Commonweal (Magazine)
Dec 17, 1999. "Forgive us our trespasses."
Author: Maurice Timothy.
Contemporary Review
May, 2000. "Christian forgiveness in Northern Ireland."
Author: Michael H. Collins.
Feeling Guilt, Finding Grace
Author: Larry K. Weeden.
Essence (Magazine)
August, 2001. "Learning to forgive and move on."
Author: Odelia Scruggs.
InfoWorld (Magazine)
April 12, 1999. "Bobby is eating humble pie - but can he afford Rose's forgiveness?"
Senior Editor: Sandy Reed.
Insight on the News (Magazine)
August 23, 1999. "An End to Violence Through Forgiveness."
(Police officer Steven McDonald and writer Johann Christoph Arnold.
Jet (Magazine)
Jan 11, 1999. "Forgiveness Boosts Health And Self-Esteem, Research Shows."
Senior Editor: Sylvia P. Flanagan.
Study Conducted by: Dr. Robert Enright.
63
Journal of Management (Magazine)
Sept., 1999. "The Effects of Blame Attributions and Offender Likableness on Forgiveness and Revenge in the Workplace.

Author: Murray Bradfield.
Ladies Home Journal (Magazine)
Nov., 2000. "Forgiveness: The Best Rx. (Effects of Grudges on Health)."
Editor: Myrna Blyth.
Learning to Forgive
Author: Doris Donnelly.
National Review (Magazine)
April 17, 2000. "ON THE RIGHT - On Forgiveness and Tolerance."
Author: William F. Buckley, Jr.
School Administrator (Magazine)
Feb., 2002. "The courage to risk forgiveness: By avoiding revenge and retribution, superintendents can nurture relationships so vital to their effectiveness."
Author: George A. Goens.
Staring Loving The Miracle of Forgiving
Author: Colleen Townsend Evans.
The Holy Bible
The Dynamics of Forgiveness
Author: James G. Emerson, Jr.
The Richest Man In Babylon
Author: George S. Clason.
USA Today (Magazine)
April, 2000. "Empathy Helps People Forgive and Forget."
Study Conducted by: Michael McCullough

Group Counseling Discussion Questions

The topics of the book itself should be used in group discussions. These questions below are to be used to help facilitate deeper group discussion and self-awareness. They should not be exclusively used as guides for discussion but as resources for helping people learn more about themselves and their behaviors.

Group Session #1, Introduction and Thesis Statement Questions
1. What are the mistakes, unresolved issues, or painful events in life that seem to continue to return to mind in your life?
2. Does my forgiveness or unforgiveness affect my anger or other emotions?
3. What are the counterproductive behaviors that I seem to continue?
4. Where do I practice the/those behavior(s)?
5. How long have I practiced the counterproductive behaviors?
6. Do I need help to overcome those counterproductive behaviors?
7. What are some of the benefits of forgiving others?
8. Is forgiving only for religious people?
9. Do you think that forgetting or pushing down the pain will make the pain go away?
10. Does it take courage to forgive?
11. Are you dealing with your past hurts, or are they dealing with you?
12. Looking back over your life, has it gotten easier or harder to forgive others?
13. Do you think or feel you are missing something?
14. Have you ever said, "I will never forgive him/her"?
15. Do you believe that God will answer your prayers if you will not forgive?

Group Session #2, Chapter 1
1. Why do you think the New Testament directs believers to confess their faults and sins?
2. Does denial of a problem help or hurt to overcome the problem?
3. Do you have a secret that affects your behavior?
4. Have your hurts from past loved ones affected your ability to connect in relationships now?
5. Have you ever disliked someone and could not understand why you did not like him/her?
6. Have you ever pushed people away without knowing why you were pushing them away?
7. Do you find yourself in the same kinds of painful relationships?
8. Do you seem to attract people with a particular kind of issues or baggage?

9. Do you try to find people in relationships who don't have particular issues, just to find out that they have those particular issues once you get into those relationships?

10. Does your frustration with people during the day affect your sleep at night?

11. Do you find yourself trying not to think about past hurts or about people who have hurt you in the past?

12. Do you feel that your unforgiveness has affected your health?

Group Session #3, Chapter 2

1. Are the people on your list from the distant past the same as the recent past?

2. How does the scripture "judge yourself and you will not be judged" relates to step two?

3. If we do not deal with the hurtful issues or baggage in our past, will it negatively affect our future?

4. If one does not recognize the painful issues (baggage), can one stop the impulses that are unconsciously driving those behaviors?

5. Do you find yourself becoming angered over insignificant problems?

6. Do the people on your list display responses to you in similar ways?

7. Do the people on this list push you away?

8. Do you push away the people on this list?

9. Is your difficulty in making good decisions the result of past hurts?

10. Do you feel you talk too much about the hurts of the past?

11. Do you feel you talk too little about the hurts of the past?

Group Session #4, Chapter 3

1. Have you asked God to help you to forgive?

2. Do you feel you need help from God to overcome the hurtful issues?

3. Do you have difficulty talking about the past?

4. Do you have difficulty remembering the past?

5. Do you become angry or sad thinking or talking about the past?

6. Do you find it hard or difficult to accept or trust people?

7. Do you find yourself reliving or remembering, over and over, the past hurtful event(s)?

8. If you feel you can't turn to God, who do you feel you can turn to?

9. Can you see the law of reciprocity applied in your life?

10. Have your past hurts caused you to behave in ways that has led to past problems, or can lead to future problems?

11. Do you feel you need to say or do things to others as to protect yourself?

12. Do you believe that your destiny has more to do with luck than your actions (hard work)?

Group Session #5, Chapter 4

1. What do you need to forgive the person for?

2. Are there smaller problems that have led up to a need to forgive this person?

3. Has someone in the past hurt you in a similar way?

4. Are there other people influencing your decision to forgive or not to forgive?

5. Is there a history of painful issues with the person you need to forgive?

Group Session #6, Chapter 5

1. Can you think of a reason why the person knowingly or unknowingly hurt you?

2. Can you think of a time when you knowingly or unknowingly hurt someone?

3. Do you think that Jesus empathized when he said, "Father forgive them, for they know not what they do"?

4. What do you think people mean when they say, "Walk a mile in their shoes"?

5. Have you said or heard someone else say that they, as kids, did not like being punished, but now they can appreciate the punishment that they received? What caused this reframing of thinking?

6. Do you think that if the children of Israel had reframed their thinking about following Moses (trusting God) in the wilderness, it would have taken forty years to get to the Promised Land?

7. Do you think you would deal with painful issues more effectively if you reframed your thinking from seeing it as a problem you have to deal with to a challenge you have to overcome?

8. Do you think it would change a teenager's feelings if you said no to buying an old, broken-down car, but said yes to a newer running car?

9. Do you think it would change the way you feel if God said no to your desires for retaliation and unforgiveness so He could say yes to your bigger desire for a healthy and happy life?

Group Session #7, Chapters 6 and 7

1. Should you only forgive those who ask for forgiveness?

2. Can you truly pray that God gives another person his best when that person has given you his or her worst?

3. Why should you pray for others to have peace in their lives when they have made your life a living hell?

(Chapter 7)

1. What do you think the scripture means when it says, "Life and death is in the power of the tongue"?

2. Can one change the way one thinks and feels?

3. Do what you and others say affect the way you feel?

4. Do you believe that the harder you yell to encourage someone, the harder he or she will try?

5. Do you believe that you can get courage from people encouraging you?
6. Do you believe that you will have less courage if others try to discourage you?

Group Session #8, Chapter 8

1. What do you think this scripture means: "Casting down imaginations, and every high thing that exalteth itself against the knowledge of God, and bringing into captivity every thought to the obedience of Christ"?
2. Are one's thoughts an indication of one's forgiveness or unforgiveness?
3. Did Jesus want the best (eternal life) for those that crucified him: "Father, forgive them, for they know not what they do"?
4. Can Jesus' forgiveness toward them be seen in his attitude toward them?
5. Can our forgiveness be seen in our attitude toward others?
6. If one's attitude toward others is to want the best for them, is there forgiveness?
7. If one's attitude toward others is that of ill will, or returning hurt for hurt, then is there forgiveness?
8. Do you think if one does not recognize the unforgiveness, then the unforgiveness will go away?

Group Session #9, Chapters 9, 10, and 11

1. Can one go through life without being offended?
2. If an alcoholic stops drinking for twenty years and then starts back after twenty years, will he/she start back as a novice drinker? Or will he/she start back where he or she stopped at twenty years ago?
3. If a person has learned to forgive but stops forgiving, will the hurts from the past stop causing self-sabotaging behaviors, or will the self-sabotaging behaviors continue?
4. What does this scripture mean: "Examine yourselves, whether ye be in the faith; prove your own selves. Know ye not your own selves" (2 Cor. 13:5)?
5. Do you see yourself as being strong? Do you see yourself as having character?

Group Session #10, Chapter 12 and Conclusion

1. Do you find yourself happier or more at peace?
2. Do you find that you are not just getting along better with the person with whom you had problems but with others as well?
3. Do you feel closer to God?
4. Do you feel like God is answering your prayers faster?
5. Do you feel like you have more faith?
6. Do you feel more spiritual?

List of Unforgiveness

Name(s)	Situation(s)	Consequences

List of Unforgiveness

Name(s)	Situation(s)	Consequences

Contact information

Michael Byrd
(817) 932-9351
pastormichaelbyrd06@gmail.com
www.pastormichaelbyrdphd.com